Who Cares Wins

How to unlock the hidden potential in people at work

Peter Savage

MERCURY

First published in hardback 1987
by Mercury Books
Published in paperback 1990
by Mercury Books
Gold Arrow Publications Ltd
862 Garratt Lane, London SW17 0NB

Set in Plantin by Phoenix Photosetting, Chatham
Printed and bound in Great Britain by
Mackays of Chatham PLC, Chatham, Kent

British Library Cataloguing in Publication Data

Savage, Peter
    Who cares wins: how to unlock the hidden
    potential in people at work.
    1. Management—Great Britain
    I. Title
    658'.00941   HD70.G7
    ISBN 1-85252-015-9

FOREWORD

It has often been stated that one of the key reasons for the decline of British industry in recent years has been the poor quality of its management.

Various explanations for this have been offered, including the fact that successive governments in the Fifties, Sixties and Seventies almost seem to have conspired with each other to punish the professional manager – subjecting him to discouragingly high rates of marginal taxation on earned income. The net result of this, of course, was that far too many of the ablest people in Britain found more rewarding outlets for their talents and enthusiasm, either abroad or through some activity in the UK where financial reward was based on capital appreciation rather than salary.

In the 1980s things started to change. At last we have a government which seems to recognise how vital it is to offer sufficient financial incentive to recruit and retain good management in British companies. There is still a long way to go, but at least a start has been made.

It is now vital that the second major argument for the poor performance of the British manager is addressed. He or she needs to be trained in a way which is fully competitive with his or her American, German or Japanese counterpart. Everyone now accepts that success in management is not achieved through divine inspiration; it requires hard work in order to master the basic skills and techniques.

Who Cares Wins represents a valuable addition to the growing library of business text books. It describes in a clear way some of the imperatives of successful management, and gives a number of examples of how these have been put into practice.

In particular, it tackles two issues which I believe lie at the heart of business success. Firstly, the recognition that customer satisfaction should be the single most important aim of all organisations, and secondly the vital importance of leadership skills to the successful manager.

SIR JOHN EGAN
Chief Executive,
British Airports Authority

ACKNOWLEDGEMENTS

I would like to thank Allan Piper, former senior editor of *International Management*, now City Writer for the Mail on Sunday, for his support and encouragement during the writing of this book.

Experience is a composite of many features and I hope I have not made reference to the work of others without acknowledgement; if I have done so it is unintentional. I would like to recognise the following works which I have referred to whilst writing this book and to which I recommend readers for further information:

In Chapter 1: *In Search of Excellence*, by Peters and Waterman, Warner Books, 1984. *The Art of Japanese Management*, by Pascale and Athos, Warner Books, 1981.

In Chapter 3: *Competitive Strategies*, by Michael Porter, The Free Press, 1980.

In Chapter 4: *Choosing Strategies for Change*, by Kotter and Schlesinger, *Harvard Business Review* No. 79202.

CONTENTS

1

THE POTENTIAL

A wind of change is blowing through the world of business and industry, yet surprisingly few of those who should be harnessing its power really understand what is happening. The change is one of style, and its effects are having tremendous impact on the way that successful companies everywhere are squaring up to the challenges of an increasingly competitive world. It's a change that has to do entirely with people, and in particular with the way that those in charge work with those they need to lead. All over Europe and the United States, just as in many of Japan's most successful corporations, managers and supervisors are learning to turn their backs on traditional management styles and look instead to the fresh approach. Behind this change is a growing realisation that in today's commercial and social climates little remains to be gained from the high-handed bossiness and managerial snobbery that has so often in the past led to worker alienation and cumbersome, self-defeating bureaucracy.

Flexibility and speed are the characteristics of today's corporate winners, and that in turn means getting the best out of every individual involved. Coercion doesn't work any more. Today's winners are those whose employees care enough to keep ahead of the opposition. And care can only be instilled into employees by the managers who lead them. It is a matter of who cares wins.

As an idea, admittedly, none of this is brand new. Climb aboard any aircraft in the United States today and chances are that half the young men and women on board will have their noses buried deep inside books on modern management. Some of these books, like *In Search of Excellence* or *The Change Makers*, have justifiably become classics but, heavy with theory, they all share a common problem: they don't explain *how* to put the theory into practice. *Who Cares Wins* is an attempt to fill that gap by showing how the actions and attitudes of ordinary managers and supervisors at all levels in the corporate hierarchy serve to shape the process of change.

Naturally enough, the commitment for change has to come from the top of any organisation: without leadership by example there can be nothing constructive to follow. But once that commitment is in place, everyone down to the shopfloor becomes an important part of the process. The change-makers are not just the high-flyers who strive for an intellectual grasp of the latest corporate-culture theories – they're the people who understand how to take the ideas and turn them into practice.

There is, unfortunately, no shortage of cynics ready to insist that such thinking is just the latest example of business school trendiness – another attempt by authors and academic thinkers to cash in on the problems of business and corporate management. Yet numerous examples exist of how the new recognition of people power, and the ability to stimulate greater involvement from employees, are having spectacular results. In many cases, companies that were once running into deep trouble have turned themselves around on the basis of nothing more than a new management style shaped simply to exploit the extra effort available in employees who previously felt alienated and out of touch with their jobs – tapping what I describe in this book as 'discretionary potential'.

When Japan's Sumitomo bought Dunlop's European tyre business in 1983, it took over from a management convinced that problems of oversupply in the market place and the easy availability of cheap imports spelt certain disaster for the tyre industry in Britain. Yet within three short years, Sumitomo turned the business around, expecting to move into profit during the fourth. The remarkable thing is that it has managed to to do it without any major investment programme and without a widespread introduction of new technology. The difference has been one of approach, and it has worked because Sumitomo is unlocking discretionary potential among its employees. Sumitomo works hard at internal communications to convey its strategies and goals clearly to everyone involved, and has adopted a style of leadership that encourages all managers to get out and about among the workforce. Productivity, in factories using the same workers and equipment previously available to Dunlop, has leapt, reaching levels Dunlop itself never came close to achieving. The effects of releasing discretionary potential are obvious.

In different ways, other companies have achieved similar successes using some or all of these techniques. Often, the key lies in developing joint identities between managers and employees, and creating a feeling that problems exist to be tackled jointly, as a team. At Avis Rent-A-Car in Britain, for example, all managers up to and including the managing director spend one week a year working on reception desks and washing cars, while employees meet their supervisors once a week to learn about the company's progress and voice their ideas or concerns about new developments and problems. Everyone stays close to corporate objectives and problems. Losing money five years ago, Avis has today established itself as the market leader in the UK, with 1986 profits in excess of $10 million. The difference between dull performance and a thriving, aggressive company, it seems, comes down to shared commitment and a joint understanding of the problems to be tackled.

There can be little doubt that wider change in many areas of management is long overdue. As markets have become increasingly international and then global, companies everywhere are being forced to face the fact that the cosy, inflexible attitudes of traditional management fail to provide the flexibility and imaginative leadership needed to beat off fierce competition. Today's winner is without question the company that knows how to use the talents of the men and women at its disposal more effectively than its competitors can use theirs. That means finding out what makes people tick, then coming to terms with giving them the room and sense of purpose to ensure they willingly give their best to the corporate good. Partly, it has to do with the advent of new technology and the greater power that it gives to individuals throughout every organisation. They have access to more information than ever before, and more often than not they may have useful ideas about how it can be used.

Rank Xerox in Britain, for example, found savings of about $1 million a year simply because it gave its invoice clerks the room to take initiatives of their own with ideas to streamline billing and recording procedures. Admittedly, the saving only counts as a small contribution to the finances of a multinational the size of Rank Xerox, but the point remains that managers who persist in stifling the creativity and enthusiasm of their employees risk overlooking tactical and strategic innovations that can make crucial differences between failure and success. Changes in social attitudes are playing their part as well, as staff and workers who might once grudgingly have accepted high-handed management styles now demand greater respect and involvement. If your company isn't providing it, you risk losing them to a competitor that will.

Building group identity and shared commitment, on the other hand, can yield spectacular results. Jaguar Cars ranks today as Britain's biggest dollar earner; of annual showroom sales around $1 billion, exports into the US market now exceed $700 million. Also it has earned a reputation fierce enough to frighten its biggest competitors, Mercedes and BMW. Yet less than ten years ago it stood on the verge of closure. How it came to be turned around is a textbook example of modern management at its best, and indeed it has become just that. The bold approach followed by Jaguar's saviour, former chairman Sir John Egan, and his visionary decision to place the responsibility for survival into the hands of everyone within the company was the key to effective change.

The kernel of the new philosophy was the responsibility of the individual – whether on the shop floor or in the office – to improve the quality of his or her work. Doing it 'right first time' as the company videos, training programmes, presentations and meetings exhorted . . . the emphasis was on workmanship and personal responsibility. To the more or less demoralised employees the vigour of the message forced new life into the company.

What makes Egan's success such a classic example of the ability to come to terms with change is his readiness not just to push responsibility on to everyone involved with Jaguar, but then to trust them completely to handle it. It implies a respect that runs from the top down as well as from the bottom up. There are no quality inspectors on Jaguar's production lines today: quality control is left to the workers themselves and to random checks by a central quality control department. Weekly meetings of workers and supervisors provide opportunities for new ideas to get an airing, and a streamlined management structure ensures that good ones are speedily implemented without unnecessary bureaucratic delays. At the same time, regular management briefings 'cascade' information down to the shop floor. One internal video shown to all workers even included confidential material on Jaguar's recently unveiled XJ6, then still at the planning stage and a product viewed crucial to the company's long-term prospects. Trust and respect have become keystones, and where Jaguar managers once feared, quite literally, to tread the shop floor, Egan encouraged them to chat with production line workers, often on first-name terms.

Even with all of this in place, of course, industrial problems are still likely to threaten any large company. The difference is that when they do arise, managers used to dealing with employees on a firm basis of trust and involvement will be better placed to handle them smoothly. Contrast the seven short days it took Jaguar to settle an industrial dispute that blew up in October 1986 with the lengthy confrontations that beset – and even characterised – its former parent British Leyland during the 1970s. Because Jaguar's employees are now driven more by clear purpose it has become easier to appeal to a sense of common good, and avoid the extremes of position-taking traditionally associated with management–union confrontation.

The point of all this is that companies like Jaguar, Xerox and Avis are finding new ways to tap more energy from their employees, all of them based on the recognition that old barriers and old snobberies – the self-destructive 'us and them' of traditional industry – have no place in today's world. That doesn't amount to a call for 'industrial socialism', the mistaken notion that because everyone has a crucial contribution to offer so everyone should expect to make strategic decisions. Decision-making and leadership still form the cornerstones of a successful enterprise. That much has already been shown by the Japanese, who first introduced the quality circles concept and from whom many of the newer ideas are springing, but who still look to hierarchical leadership for ultimate guidance. The difference is one of trust and a recognition that getting people to identify with company goals gives them a sense of purpose that leads them willingly to provide the extra energy every company needs in its bid for success – their 'discretionary potential'.

An interesting example of how this can work comes from a recent period of British history – the Falklands War, which pitted British troops against Argentine soldiers during the early summer of 1982. While the rights and wrongs of the conflict still provoke sharp political controversy, the sense of purpose it generated in some quarters was nothing short of remarkable. The workforce of one engineering company on the south coast, contracted to build a helideck during the temporary conversion of the liner QE2 into a troopship, astonished its management by completing the job in two days flat, against the two weeks it might normally have taken. Yet within a few months, with the war over and the sense of binding purpose gone, productivity reverted to previous stand-ards. What changed was simply that sense of purpose gave way to self-interest and pursuit of personal gain. The task now is to find ways of reigniting that brief spark of energetic endeavour, and using it to kindle a lasting commitment to long-term growth. Many Britons took a great deal of pride in their achievements while the conflict lasted without stopping to ask why they could not extend their brief efforts into their normal, everyday, working lives: they took pride in their achievement, but find no shame in the norm.

It's not difficult to understand, on the other hand, how morale-sapping production-line methods and multinational bureaucra-cies have over time helped nurture attitudes like these. As com-panies became bigger and relied increasingly on mass-production techniques so they progressively lost touch with the very people they depended on to produce their profits – their employees. At the same time, the employees themselves came no longer to identify with the products they turned out or with the people who employed them. In companies like British Leyland, etc., the effects have been obvious in years of declining profits, endless rounds of industrial strife and, often, ultimate failure. How America's newly successful corporations reversed that process is shown by Peters and Waterman in their classic *In Search of Excellence*, with the now famous list of eight criteria operated by all 43 of the top multinationals they studied. The winners, they found, are those that:

- Stay close to their customers.
- Stick to the knitting (i.e. stay with what they know best).
- Operate a simple form (i.e. keep their hierarchies simply to allow communication).
- Are hands on–value driven (i.e. keep close to their employees, and encourage strong corporate identity, with firm leadership).
- Allow autonomy/entrepreneurship (i.e. structure themselves to allow employee-independence).
- Have a bias for action (i.e. act instead of over-analysing options).
- Are simultaneously loose and tight (i.e. have a dedication to central values but tolerate latitude around those values).
- Achieve productivity through people (i.e. instil a sense of shared purpose into employees).

Taking these eight criteria, it's interesting to note two outstanding points. The first is that studies of successful Japanese companies show they exhibit similar features to those identified by Peters and Waterman in US corporations. The similarities suggest that both in Japan and the US top companies have separately identified the same key features of success. In their book *The Art of Japanese Management*, Pascale and Athos found seven features (the 7 S's) prevalent in successful Japanese companies:

- Strategy (close to customers; stick to knitting)
- Structure (simple form)
- Systems (hands on–value driven)
- Style (autonomy-entrepreneurship)
- Skills (bias for action)
- Staff (simultaneous loose-tight)
- Shared purpose (productivity through people)

7

The second point, notable about both lists, is that most of the criteria concern the way that companies operate internally – the way they relate to their employees. Of the eight features identified by Peters and Waterman, only the first two focus on external objectives. Companies which succeed are those that (*a*) listen to their customers and (*b*) stick to the business they know best. These two features coincide with the first of the 7 S's. But in both the US and Japanese cases, all the remaining features have to do with internal organisation and behaviour. The lesson is clear: superior performance springs largely from a real recognition of the importance of the people who make any company run smoothly – its employees.

If any doubts remain, a good way to test them is by considering a list of rules that might be found in companies doing the opposite from those listed by *In Search of Excellence* or those following the 7 S's. Such a list might well be entitled *In Search of Mediocrity*, and almost certainly includes items embarrassingly familiar to many of today's managers:

- Bias against action (multi-layered repetitive reviews of any idea).

- Far from customers (don't listen to them; don't show any loyalty; use changing price incentives to keep business).

- Central control, low risk (don't allow initiative from below; discourage expression of ideas; don't risk making mistakes; run tight departments with few task groups; operate tight job descriptions).

- Low people productivity (don't stimulate common purpose; don't show employer commitment; keep flexibility out, and allow change only through negotiations).

- Hands-off, imposed culture (operate formal conservative organisation; provide high perks for top management, then negotiate through unions; keep top management aloof and out of sight, usually behind closed doors; don't expect employee feedback, and never act on it).

- Unnecessary diversification (regardless of skill requirements).

- Complex form, top heavy (leave people to do jobs beneath

them; try to control people with supervisors instead of facilitating action; keep things bureaucratic – us and them).

- Control heavy and tight (don't allow freedom; keep everyone thinking the same; don't tolerate different approaches; use detailed rules to run everything).

It is refreshingly surprising how far some company leaders have already been prepared to go to put that kind of approach behind them in order to create the environment that leads to high performance. SAS Chairman Jan Carlssen is widely recognised as one of Europe's top chief executives for his achievement in turning the airline into a world beater. In his early days at the controls, Carlssen approached one of his managers to ask how much investment might be needed in his area to meet the new corporate objectives. When the manager suggested the likely figure, Carlssen astonished him by authorising it there and then – no reports, no interminable meetings, no threat of recrimination, just a straightforward trust in the abilities and judgement of people working as part of a team. At the end of the day the necessary work was completed well under the estimated figure as people responded to this new style.

SAS today exhibits all the characteristics of a high-performance company, chief among them *clearly stated direction, lean form* and *flexible people*. The company has goals to which management is committed, it believes people work better when they are clearly motivated, and – crucially – it recognises that it is people who change companies. Carlssen is just one of a growing group of chief executives who recognise the six key benefits of high performance:

- Output exceeds usual standards.
- It exceeds what your competitors can do.
- It uses fewer resources.
- It exceeds expected potential.
- It creates an outstanding image.
- It becomes a source of inspiration.

At the same time, it's important to recognise that different

9

people achieve high performance in different ways: there is no one best way of getting there. For any individual, high performance springs from 'the set of conditions under which I do things extremely well'. Helping people to find those conditions depends on helping them understand themselves – their strengths, weaknesses and needs. Various analytical techniques are available, but the important thing is to recognise that translating individual high performance into group high performance depends critically on open, honest communication. Allowing and encouraging people, workers and managers alike, to express their personal concerns and needs will ensure that more people end up in jobs that really suit them, and where they feel valued. As a result, they will start building on their own strengths and contributing to the company as a whole. Creating high performance at the individual level, in short, allows its translation to group and, ultimately, organisation level. The basis steps are simple enough:

- Encourage innovation – don't punish failure but try to learn from it.
- Get in touch – wander about, use simple methods of control, look for feedback and work in small task groups.
- Stay close to customers – listen to them, innovate with them, don't break promises.
- Show your own commitment – trust and delegate, share information and recognise there is very little that can't be said. Train people properly. Say 'thank you'.
- Install unique values – provide clear vision, measure performance, have fun, celebrate success and find champions.

Now let's see how to put this into practice. . . .

2

HOW TO CHANGE:
THE OVERALL PROCESS

We've looked briefly at high performance and what it means to organisations, groups and individuals and we've seen the results arising from its achievement. Most of us already know there are better ways of working – more effective or more efficient – but what is our usual frustration? It is not being able to see *how* to change, how to start the process, how to foster it and how to achieve the results we know are possible. So how have others managed to achieve success, what are the lessons to be learned?

The following chapters describe the process of creating effective and successful change. Each organisation is unique in terms of its need for change and the changes required. Equally, its own stage of development is peculiar to itself – what is the management style, how clear are its business goals, how motivated are its employees. It is quite impossible therefore to predetermine the precise steps of a successful change programme. However, it is possible and practical to establish the process required to implement such a programme. Where and how you will start will greatly depend on your own organisation's needs and its stage of development, but the entire process will look like the chart overleaf and this provides an effective checklist against which to decide actions and measure progress.

We shall now look at each of these steps in more detail in the following chapters:

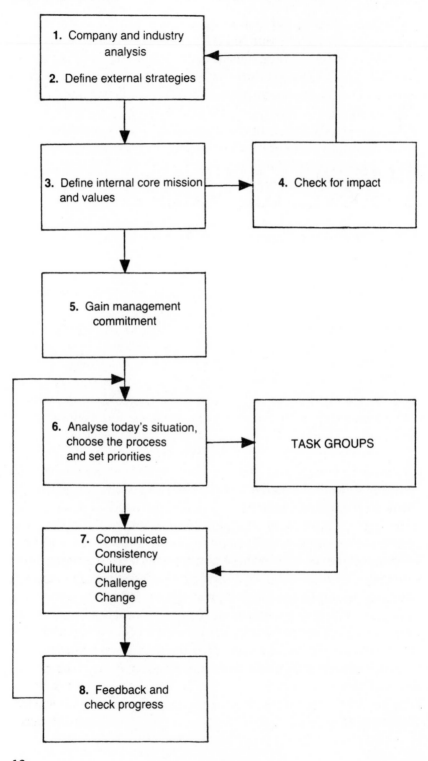

1. Company and industry analysis
2. Define external strategies

3. Define internal core mission and values

4. Check for impact

5. Gain management commitment

6. Analyse today's situation, choose the process and set priorities

TASK GROUPS

7. Communicate
   Consistency
   Culture
   Challenge
   Change

8. Feedback and check progress

The next chapter will look at steps 1, 2, 3 and 4 – seeing where your company fits in your industry, assessing its strengths and weaknesses and defining where it is going. These first steps require clear understanding *before* major internal change is started. The management has to know where it is going and be able to convince others!

Most companies attempt this process only to stop halfway; they do not identify or express that central binding purpose which pulls people in and gains their commitment. Without a core mission or purpose, an organisation can still become very *efficient*; the difference is that without this binding purpose *effectiveness* will never be achieved.

To explain this difference, let us look at a simple drawing:

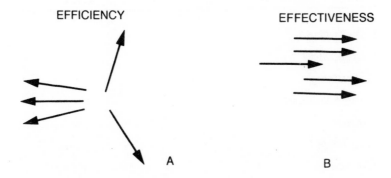

The first picture shows five departments in an *efficient* company; the second drawing five departments in an *effective* company. The step from efficiency to effectiveness is made by finding the common purpose to which people can align so that everyone pulls in one direction. An *efficient* Accountancy Department, for example, provides excellent data on time for the Board to run the company. An *effective* Accountancy Department not only provides the Board with this service, it helps the salesman, the production foreman and other people to do *their* jobs better, by providing them with data suitable to meet their own needs.

Efficiency and effectiveness have external impact too: the model T Ford was made by a very *efficient* manufacturing process, at its time far better than any of Ford's competitors. Yet the car lost its market because Ford did not recognise quickly enough the need for choice in colours and style. They stayed too long with 'you can have any colour as long as its black'. It had efficiency but not effectiveness – it started to lose sales to its competitors.

Chapter 4 will then outline how today's situation in an organisation can be analysed so that the choice of the process for change can be made. Varying change processes will be described, and one will fit your situation best. This chapter describes the process and then shows how priorities can be established quickly with a high degree of involvement.

The subsequent chapters then set out the internal change process itself. The company direction and external strategies will have been established; a purpose will have been defined as to why the organisation is in being; you will have made decisions on which process of change to institute; and now the internal change process can start. This is established around the seven C's:

- *Core purpose*
- *Commitment*
- *Consistency*
- *Communication*
- *Culture*
- *Challenge*
- *Change*

and a chapter is devoted to each, together with ideas on how to start the process and the overall probability of success.

3

THE CHANGE PROCESS – FIRST STEPS

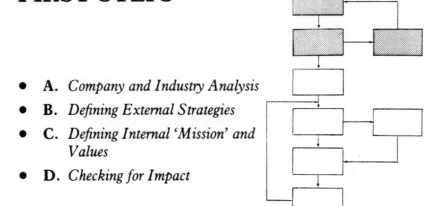

- **A.** *Company and Industry Analysis*
- **B.** *Defining External Strategies*
- **C.** *Defining Internal 'Mission' and Values*
- **D.** *Checking for Impact*

A. *Company and Industry Analysis*

Before initiating internal change the company must have a sound business direction which is understood by its leaders. It must be realistic, sensible and viable and this requires understanding of the company, its competition and its industry. This basic under-standing of the company and its position is absolutely the key, not only from a business standpoint but also, as we shall see, from the standpoint of convincing others inside the company to commit to the company.

A suggested technique is **SWOP analysis**, which critically looks at your industry and your company within it:

Company	*Industry*
Strengths	**O**pportunities
Weaknesses	**P**roblems

15

The data for this analysis can come from your own (internal) assessments but you can also use external help – industry studies or consultants – to ensure you are not blinkered.

Asking a customer to provide an assessment of you as a supplier and asking him to *compare* you with others is not only a superb technique for helping this SWOP analysis, it also provides a fund of information on how you can specifically improve your customer service *and* gives you insights into your competition's performance, goals and skills. An added bonus is that most customers are delighted to be asked, enjoy the process and will provide you with some very direct marketing feedback. A process worthwhile in its own right! Indeed, as we shall see later, regular opinion surveys internally provide a barometer of the company and help measure the effectiveness of change; similar outside customer surveys can do as much good to quantify the external effectiveness of a company, its service and its products.

So first check what is happening to the industry:
     Analyse its environment and growth;
     Assess the competition;
and then Assess your own company's strengths and weaknesses.

Next question what your business is doing now: where will your current strategies take you; what will be the competition's responses; does the industry outlook fit your strategies?

Then reassess what your business should be doing: what are the possible strategic choices and what are the *best* strategies? Do these fit into your assessment of where the industry is going?

In the industry analysis you will look at its overall profitability. This is determined by several features:

* The power of suppliers to it.

* The power of customers.

* Potential substitutes to your products.

* Who are the competition – what is their share?

* How easy is it for newcomers to enter?

* How easy is it for leavers to leave?

• What is the cost structure of the product(s)?

- What effect will new technology have?
- What is the differentiation of products in the market?
- What is the overall profitability of the market?
- What is the growth rate of the industry?

Your aim is to understand overall profitability and the key factors affecting the industry, then you can relate your own company to it by asking the same questions of yourself:

- What is your competitive position?
- What is your market share?
- How will your share change?
- Do you have unique advantages/disadvantages?
- What are your own cost structures?

Your aim is to find the *position* where you can best exploit your strengths and defend yourself against competition.

In the overall industry analysis the items starred ★ represent the key elements which determine overall profitability – powerful sellers/buyers, easy substitutable products, intense rivalry, high exit barriers and low entry barriers all create a low profitability industry. This is usually exemplified by commodity products with little differentiation between individual competitors' products. Michael Porter's *Competitive Strategy* is an excellent reference book to guide the process of industry and competitive assessment, and contains more detail of much of the summary given here. It is essential reading for this phase of work.

B. *Defining External Strategies*

In response to the industry, competitive and own-company analysis, there are three main strategies that can be followed:

- Cost leadership
- Product differentiation
- Focus

In general-purpose, undifferentiated products (such as commodities) **cost leadership** is essential. Every product can acquire speciality status, even commodities; however, this is generally through the service provided rather than by the product itself whose features are not readily discernible from another producer's product.

The **risks** to the cost leadership strategy are often caused through over-emphasis on manufacturing rather than marketing. Also technology change can suddenly wipe out your advantage, as happened to the conventional wind-up clock industry when battery-powered clocks and watches suddenly appeared. It happened in turn to these battery-powered watches when the small stud-battery digital watches arrived.

The effects of inflation and the learning curve in manufacture can combine rapidly to erode your advantage. The learning curve of a product represents the cost savings that will occur as production volume accumulates. For some products the effect can be as large as 4–5 per cent per annum. So the highest-volume commodity producer keeps ahead of his competition by making more units at less and less unit cost. But others can follow down the same cost curve, and care that *you* continue progress down the curve is essential. The pack will catch you if you stand still.

Differentiation is the strategy choice when your product can be distinguished from the competition by some unique feature. The product range can then be sold – often at a price premium – as the competition's products have become unwanted or unusable.

The risks to this strategy are imitation of the 'unique' properties by others; also the market need for differentiation may decline, or the cheaper cost of other products may outweigh the benefits of differentiation in the customers' eyes.

Probably the best example of the risks of differentiation is the UK motorcycle industry. It used to be the largest in the world; now it is non-existent. The decay began in the 1950s when Japanese bikes with cost leadership began to appear in the small bike market – 50, 100 up to 200 cc models. The home industry could not compete and so withdrew to larger bike manufacture – 350, 500, 650 cc, etc. – in the belief they could differentiate their products from the new Japanese products. What happened? With a volume base established in the market, the Japanese attacked the larger bike market segments and took them too, because there was no genuine differentiation. The sad result is that there no longer is a UK industry with those famous names – BSA, Norton, Villiers, Triumph, etc.

The third major strategy is **focus**. This is generally found when a company concentrates on a specific geographic area or end-user market. Again the risks are clear: sub-markets can arise or cost leadership by others can be used as a tool to encroach on the focused market. The motorcycle market in the UK also provides a prime example in this category. The domestic producers focused on the UK rather than world market, and made themselves highly vulnerable to other competitors entering 'their' market, particularly as those new competitors had cost leadership through their very high volumes in other world markets.

Choices between the three key business strategies have to be made, and it is possible to combine two or all three. The secret is an understanding of what your strategy is and to ensure it is viable. Declining industries often opt for cost leadership as the market is mature and new differentiation or focus is difficult to find; nevertheless, even in the most mature industries entrepreneurial marketing can find the opportunities – no product is a pure commodity except in the eye of the poor producers!

In the assessment of industry and the competition, it is significant to determine the competitor's chosen strategy, as it will determine his reaction to yours. Many businesses have failed because they have been stuck in the middle between all three strategies or were unaware of the key driving strategies of their competition.

The last stage of your strategy assessment is to understand the 'life-phase' of your product. There are four phases and their features are illustrated on page 20.

Each phase requires a different environment and different skills to optimise the product's life and profitability. Creating the idea, growing the market, beating the competition, squeezing the declining product's cash flow by minimum cost operations – four completely different skills. You reward people who achieve what is required; how do you reward these four different skills with a standard reward system?

	CREATION	GROWTH	MATURITY	DECLINE
AIM	FIND OPPORTUNITY	DEVELOP IT	GAIN	OPTIMISE
SKILL NEEDED	INNOVATION	MARKETER	STRATEGIST	OPERATOR
MEASURED BY	NEW BUSINESS	GROWTH	RELATIVE	RETURN
ORGANISATION	LOOSE ⟶			TIGHT

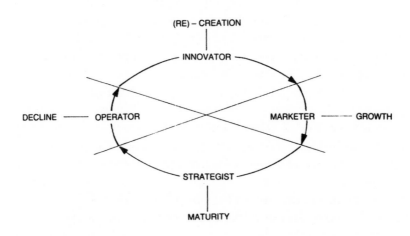

Failure to understand the life-cycle stage very often happens in large companies whose diversity of business portfolio is not recognised in company culture or reward systems. In the late 1970s the basic petrochemical industry in Europe was already in its decline phase with volume beginning to fall off. Yet several of the key companies involved were still acquiring competitors and trying to *expand* their business as if the market was in its growth phase. The result of not appreciating which phase the industry was in was a major contribution to a nett loss peaking at two billion dollars a year for the European industry. Since the pain became so acute, reality has been seen and some 20 per cent of the industry's capacity has disappeared – a true reflection of the stage of decline but a costly consequence of the failure to understand the product's cycle until it was too late.

So the art of leadership is to guide the product's phasing in terms of supportive needs and to prepare the environment for the product's *next* phase. The way the business is accounted needs to change through the life cycle, the rewards for personnel should change as the aims change and the structure of the organisation and investment strategy will alter. Yet how many of our companies, particularly the larger ones, are able to exist with more than one phase, in management attitude, control and leadership, within their organisations? Reward systems are standardised across the entire company, ignoring the very different needs of a creative business compared with a declining one. Perhaps this is one of the key weaknesses of the large multi-national: it is as yet unable to cope with the multitude of business systems required properly to run many diverse sub-businesses. (We return to this theme under the change programme itself.) Within this concern the hardest element is recreating innovation – particularly when the company is in the 'tight' declining product stage; leaders can not let go enough to release their people's innovative skills and develop new opportunities. The environment stifles the entrepreneurial flair. How many companies recently have publicly bemoaned their lack of innovation? Chances are their environment, from reward to recruitment, is firmly established to discourage innovation!

C. *Defining Internal Mission and Values*

The analysis so far will have enabled you to understand your industry, your competition, your products' life-cycle position and to have selected the best external strategies for your products and organisation. You will have recycled the strategy choice to ensure it is viable within the industry. This external strategy now needs to be 'internalised' – to be represented in a way that is meaningful to employees.

The product life-phase analysis will already have yielded many clues as to what this means inside the company – as will your strategy choice. The key question to address is: 'If my strategies and plans are successful, what will the company look like in five to ten years time?'

An effective way of addressing this question and at the same time to begin the process of involving and committing others to the direction of the company is to open this issue up to a group of the senior executives in the organisation. In small companies or autonomous units of bigger companies this could be made very exciting and rewarding by involving *all* the management of the company. To be effective the group's maximum number should be limited to 12 people; above that level 'air time' or contribution time becomes limited to the point where some may be present without feeling involved.

Have the initial external industry and competitive analysis carried out by a senior executive or even a small group of people. The charting of the company's strengths, weaknesses, opportunities and problems will take time but it is unlikely to provoke extremes of opinions. The choice of company strategies is obviously more contentious and this will involve the leadership's input. So, before starting the first meeting with management the analysis needs to be prepared and at least the outline of the strategies formulated.

The management group should be assembled away from the work environment for an entire day – possibly two. The outside venue tends to break 'work rules' of behaviour and the location should be relaxed to try to achieve highest participation – perhaps a dinner the evening before to set the scene and deformalise the event; casual clothes to signify the badges of authority are to be diluted; perhaps a guest speaker of an inspirational or challenging nature to set the tone of the atmosphere you are trying to generate on the day.

The first part of the day will be the presentation of the analysis. Allow time for clarification and invite participants to take exception, but this will nevertheless be a fairly straightforward exercise. Then the leader will, using the analysis as a data platform, show the external strategy direction he sees for the company and the resultant company strategies.

Again, allow time for additions and deletions; this part will involve more discussion but time must be allowed for the group to agree, identify with and feel a part of, the modifications and the finally agreed strategies.

An example is the process Scandinavian Airline System (SAS) went through a few years ago. Their industry analysis would have shown their market share in Europe, assessed the size of travel growth through to 1990, and looked at their competitors, assessing their strengths and weaknesses (Lufthansa on punctuality, Swissair on service, etc.). They concluded that business travel was the growth sector of the market with the best margins and then assessed what was needed to be number one in this market. Service, punctuality, professionalism, reliability were the key needs to serve this market and SAS embarked on a deep programme to become number one – in their chosen strategic direction. That it has been successful owes much to the identification of the correct strategy and then as much to their internal commitment to align and commit all their workforce to this goal: to provide the best business travel service in Europe.

When the strategy is clear, the group needs to decide its key mission or purpose and describe it in a way that is clear and meaningful to everyone (e.g. to be the best business travel service in Europe).

Having achieved this, the group then needs to set out what the company will look like in five to ten years' time with this mission. What will be needed to achieve it, what will be the organisation, the information needs, the business structure, the reward systems and what values will be paramount to achieve this. This *vision* of the future is the key in transmitting the needs through the company together with the values and the environment which will need to be established.

Again with the SAS example, the key words of service, punctuality, reliability already start to state the values to be held dear. Friendly, courteous helpful staff must be a prerequisite, which in turn means competence and everyone being aware of the paramount need to support the positive atmosphere to customers. Contrast some other airlines, where most requests are too much trouble and you leave a flight feeling you are a seat number rather than the customer. SAS very quickly established the simple values of service to be paramount and woe betide those who acted against them; these values were protected at all costs.

So this exercise will provide a business aim, but just as important will describe the values the company will operate by. With these agreed, it will be easy to find the company's main mission or purpose. It will not be just to make money; it will have a purpose relating to others – i.e.

- The best . . .
- The highest quality . . .
- The best customer service . . .
- The first to develop . . .

The purpose must be challenging and exciting enough to enable people to buy in and commit to it. It's probably this already, it only needs expression; indeed, an organisation with no purpose will have little internal commitment and will inevitably decay.

Challenging and involving the top management in joining in this process begins the commitment process. It will also rapidly show that the core of the organisation – the structure, culture, skills, rewards, investment analysis, accounting methods – will probably all have to change. Any feature of an organisation unchanged for ten or twenty years is likely to be inadequate for the next ten or twenty years. Yet how many of our companies do their business in the same way as twenty years ago? The key Government departments, the Civil Service, have an unchanged reward system. Little wonder then that innovation and new methods fail to live in such a structured static world.

This process of strategically analysing the company and then defining its direction, key purpose or mission and values lies at the heart of the change process. Until it is completed and the top management is totally comfortable with it, the internal change process cannot be started. Whether the process takes three months or three years, this base has to be established before moving on.

D. *Checking for Impact*

After defining the organisation's mission or purpose and values, it is necessary to go back to the external strategy industry analysis. Is the mission realistic and relevant? Are the key business strategies and company purpose compatible? They will surely be so if

24

the process is followed; however, the recycle is worthwhile before the next stage of opening up the conclusions to others in the organisation. They will be questioned and challenged and the preparation of the recycle is necessary. This process is one which the whole workforce will feel the *management* has to lead. They will expect it to be thoroughly undertaken; after all, it paves the way the company is going to tread for the next decade.

Summary

We have now analysed the industry, the competitors, and your own company; defined the external business or product strategies; and then 'internalised' the process to define a purpose for the company and a set of values it wishes to operate by to achieve the purpose. Finally, a check has been made that the elements are compatible. Now we are prepared to tackle the internal change process. Let's see how this is carried out. . . .

4

ANALYSIS OF TODAY'S SITUATION

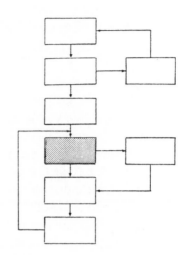

- ● **A.** *Choosing the Process*
- ● **B.** *Setting Priorities*

A. *Choosing the Process*

There is no one right choice of internal change process. However, the choice must be deliberate and will depend entirely on the factors in your particular organisation. Kotter and Schlesinger (*Choosing Strategies for Change*) analysed the methods available and these can be simply summarised:

Method	*Effectiveness*
● Involvement	Positive, irreversible, slow
● Negotiation	Expensive, reversible, power balance?
● Manipulation	Crisis, commitment low, fast
● Coercion	Forced, reversible, fastest

If a company is in dire straights, there may be no time for an involved committed change process, and coercion or manipulation are used because they are fastest. However, these methods are highly reversible in their efficiency gain as commitment has not been given: a temporary use has probably been made of

27

management's strength. Once used, the day will come when the pendulum will swing away and much, if not most, of the gain may be lost. Nevertheless, coercion is a technique that has been used by much of British industry since 1980, due to the depressed conditions and the need to do something urgently.

The Rover Group, British Steel and the Coal Board are prime examples of the crisis reaction with a test of strength to achieve results. Although the first two have since moved up the method scale and are now more actively trying to involve their workforces, the risk of reversion will inevitably remain high.

The higher end of the method scale leads to high performance, where the time is taken to commit employees to the company's aim and purpose and commitment is *given* by those employees. At this end of the scale the process is much less reversible and in the longer run far more effective.

Jaguar, whilst again starting low on the method scale because of the crisis facing the company and the need for urgent action, have moved swiftly up the scale in an attempt to make permanent the efficiency gains captured. This has been achieved by involvement of the workforce, particularly in the key theme of *quality*. Quality was a serious problem in the 1970s. The common US story that if you wanted a Jaguar you must have two – one for use on the road and one for spares – was a reflection of perceived product quality. The rapid change to the vehicle selling on its quality again has required the entire workforce to recognise the problem, be involved in its solution, and be committed to quality achievement. This radical revision to pre-war standards of work would have been unforeseeable in 1980.

At the highest end of the scale there are, lamentably, all too few British companies. The clearest examples of total commitment to high performance are seen mainly in US, European and Japanese companies. Scandinavian Airline Systems (SAS), McDonalds, IBM and many others bear witness to such achievements and their reward. All these companies set out to become the best in their industry and took the time and effort to ensure all the workforce felt the purpose was worthwhile and contributed to the process.

The choice of process is influenced by the need for speed balanced against the need for irreversible effectiveness and commitment. If there is any choice, the latter must dominate, as organisations seek excellence and competitive edge permanently –

transitional performance means little. However, crisis will always force some to demand rapid change and risk reversibility.

The two steps involved in making the process choice – the need for speed and the need for permanence – have a third element: understanding **resistance**. Resistance to change may well play a major role in the process choice.

Kotter and Schlesinger found four main types of resistance:

- 1 Self interest
- 2 Misunderstanding
- 3 Different assessment of benefits
- 4 Low tolerance

Lets look at these briefly in turn:

1. Self-interest is quite obvious and very common. At higher levels it is often the career *v.* company issue which surfaces. Change can be a threatening process, and those keenest to maintain the status quo are likely to be at higher levels – after all they have succeeded within the existing rules and methods, so why change! We recognise the self-interest of unionised groups where the commitment to the union may be higher than to the company, but it is often as overtly true in management positions. Protection of status, perks and privileges is often as strongly fought as are demarcations on the shop floor, and professional demarcations are equally strongly protected – sometimes even by law! The level of self-interest in a company requires understanding before a change programme is embarked upon.

2. Misunderstanding is always a resistance builder. Time has to be allowed in communicating to enable people to understand the need for change. This gestation time varies but it can be up to several years before people will even trust the information given, if the organisation has had a history of inconsistent and poor management, or little communication.

3. Different assessment of the benefits of change is a high resistance builder. If the result of improved productivity is to lose jobs in a workgroup, the group's resistance to that productivity will be high. Remember when you were punished as a child only to be told that 'this hurts me more than it hurts you'; you had a

29

different assessment as the receiver! This demands that management find new ways of utilising time created by productivity improvements, hopefully by producing more products but perhaps also by reducing purchases in services or retraining people into scarcer skill areas. Have someone look at what you purchase from outside: it will truly amaze you how much you are spending and how many people are employed. If this process is not enough to absorb the productivity change, consider reversing the process and contracting out your spare skills: you'll be surprised by the income generated.

This thinking applies to both groups and individuals. A sign of rigid and wasteful thinking recently has been the numbers released through early retirement without a thought for contracting them out, except by a few companies (ICI, BP for example). The wastage of skills is enormous and the indignity of the process a source of irritation at best and cynicism at worst, both in the whole company watching the process and for those directly involved. Commitment is unlikely in an organisation that scraps its elder citizens – precipitating them in an undignified process onto a 'no use here' scrap heap.

4. Low tolerance level is abundant in us all; fear of the unknown is always strong. Allow time for people to adapt, allow escape routes and reversible experiments – show there is a way out of the problems. Management's own style in this is critical; the example of unpunished failure is the key to success. Allow people to see that life is like riding the wing of an aeroplane – a new sport where the golden rule for survival is 'don't let go of one hold until you are sure of the next'!

Considering the four resistances types is important in assessing your change method. Consider the political leadership of our country and why it has continually failed. We all exhibit the resistance features, and without professional communications, consistency and, above all, the gestation period, it is not too surprising we've moved very little forward as a country in terms of commitment, except in times of crisis when real and obvious purpose suddenly briefly reappears. Our political process is too inconsistent, the politicians' ability to communicate too restricted and the time taken to allow full understanding too short to overcome the population's natural resistance.

To sum up, a simple scorecard of assessment will provide a

guide to which of the change options best suit your own need:

Resistance level and types	Low score 0	High score 5
Management commitment	Low score 0	High score 5
Management's dependence on others	Low score 0	High score 5
Need for speed	Low score 5	High score 0
Need for irreversibility	Low score 0	High score 5

TOTAL

Assess your organisation on a scale of 0 to 5 for each element as shown. The higher you score, the more you are driven to high performance at the highest end of the change process – through involvement. This book describes this end of the spectrum only: if you score less than 9, stop reading now. This book does not attempt to teach coercion or manipulation: it is about high performance through a committed workforce and management.

B. *Setting Priorities*

From your strategic analysis and the mission work you will be able to describe the company and some of the environment features that you are seeking. A novel way to set priorities is to take the physical description you have derived and write down in more detail, in single descriptive words or phrases, the working environment you are seeking. This effectively becomes a list of the *values* you feel will be important for the organisation to succeed. Having done this, write down the opposites of these words or phrases. With a 0–100 range, then have key managers in your company plot where they feel you are today. The resulting averaged profile will quickly show where you have most need for change.

An example follows taking some of the criteria of high performance that will probably have emerged from your own analysis of the environment and values needed to achieve your 5–10 year mission.

The plot shown overleaf indicates that 'risks', 'common values' and 'challenging' are the areas where most progress needs to be

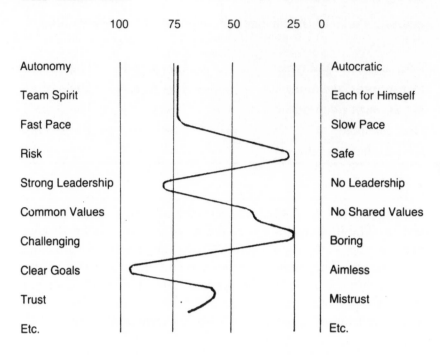

	100	75	50	25	0	
Autonomy						Autocratic
Team Spirit						Each for Himself
Fast Pace						Slow Pace
Risk						Safe
Strong Leadership						No Leadership
Common Values						No Shared Values
Challenging						Boring
Clear Goals						Aimless
Trust						Mistrust
Etc.						Etc.

made, i.e. where today you are furthest from the internal environment and values you seek, and need, to achieve your mission. As time progresses, wider opinion surveys can be used to produce data to guide the process. However, initially it will be best to use the same senior management group assembled to work on the mission (in Chapter 3).

After this plot has been made, it is a simple task to turn the priority areas into actions and at the same time involve others lower in the organisation. Again as an example, after the senior management meetings described in Chapter 3, set up similar sized groups at the next level down in the company. Repeat the process, i.e.

(a) Describe your assessment of the company, the industry and your competitors.

(b) Describe the strategic direction you have identified.

(c) Describe the vision of where the company will be in the future and the type of environment and the key values that vision will entail.

(d) Allow time for these new groups to question the results of (a), (b) and (c) and then request their help by setting down the continuum you see for your own company.

(e) Ask the group individually to assess where they feel the organisation is today on the continuum and average all the plots to find the consensus 'scores'.

(f) Now split the group into subgroups and ask them to address those areas furthest from tomorrow's needs (i.e. perhaps those with scores of below 60).

They can best carry out this last step by first giving examples of why the particular score is low, and then describing what needs to be done to improve it. Tell them to tackle the problems by asking:

- How to ………
  or
- I wish that ………

The groups will then concentrate on defining what needs to be done rather than concentrating on today's (poor) situation. Often the phrase 'I wish that' will indicate where to go and 'How to' will describe what needs to be done to achieve the goal.

As an example if **trust** scores 20 per cent on your own continuum:

- I wish that ……… our people did a full day's work.

  ……… our people only took one hour for lunch.

  ……… tea breaks were only ten minutes.

  ……… we could trust men to fill in their own time sheets.

  ……… we did not have to administer overtime.

- How to   ……… start work promptly.

  ……… stop lunch overrunning.

  ……… get rid of fixed tea breaks.

  ……… get time sheets self-accounted.

  ……… get overtime accountable by those who work it.

These type of lists identify issues of mistrust and they start to indicate what needs to be done to achieve more trust. By questioning in this positive way the listing becomes a goal rather than a bitch list of what is wrong today. Those listings of 'I wish' and 'How to' themselves become work action items by definition *and* in the process you have increased identity, ownership and commitment of all those involved in the exericse – it becomes '*our* problem and challenge' instead of *yours*.

If, as is likely, the groups develop a list of priority areas too big to handle, give each member a notional £5 to 'spend' and ask him to put his money beside the issues most important to him. Adding up the 'money' against each item will readily enable you to identify areas of greatest concern and therefore where most energy is. These items should be worked first.

Besides this type of exercise the organisation will also have pre-defined priority areas – perhaps relating to the external environment and the business itself. Nevertheless, this same simple technique can be usefully employed in these areas also.

By tackling these problems in this way you can use the small task groups to work on the priority areas. You may well wish to use those who voted the most money to an area to work on that area as they will have the most energy and interest in finding solutions. They should be allowed to operate as task groups for a defined time (perhaps a month) to propose solutions where possible, recycle to management – who should agree the proposals or not – and then action them and pass on to new tasks. Keep the process alive and keep it moving. After the first group has reported back and action has been *seen*, the commitment of the next group will be larger and so the process repeats. Lack of action kills the process; if this happens it will be management's fault, so *commitment* to action is needed from day one.

So here is a simple method of setting priorities, not dictating them, which will widen involvement and commitment to change and build confidence in the change process.

Now let us look at the change process itself.

5

THE CHANGE ELEMENTS

The Seven C's

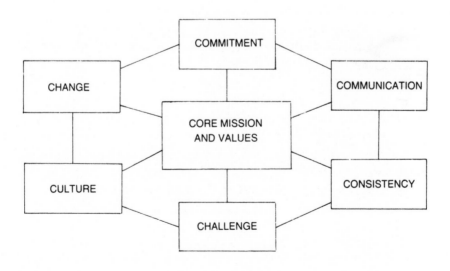

The seven C's are all linked through the company's purpose and values; without this link progress will be ponderous and highly reversible. Indeed, if the company has no clear purpose and values, it is probably better not to read further as the change process is highly transparent and will quickly be seen to have no purpose for people to align to and support.

The seven elements are all intertwined and all depend on each other; failure at any one will threaten all the others. Success depends on the recognition of each element and its inter-relationship with the others. We shall now examine the key elements in *turn*.

6

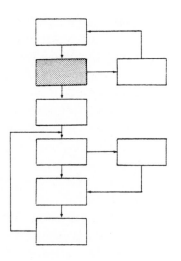

CORE PURPOSE: MISSION AND VALUES

The mission (or purpose) will have been identified earlier in the process (Chapter 3). Many companies have found their purpose by expressing their overall goal – often with reference to the competition: to be *the best* in quality or service or to be the number one innovators. This simple statement of purpose often becomes the driving force for change and progress in the company's fortunes. Some examples are shown below:

Company	Purpose	Issue
IBM	IBM Means Service	Service
Chubb Insurance	Underwriting Excellence	Quality
Leo Burnett	Make Great Adverts	Quality
General Electric	Progress is Our Most Important Product	Innovation
Sears Robuck	Quality at a Good Price	Market segment
Dana Corp.	Productivity Through People	People
NASA	A Man on the Moon by the End of the Decade	Mission

(This list is extracted from *In Search of Excellence* by Peters and Waterman.)

It's no coincidence that no British companies are listed: examples of a true corporate purpose are hard to find in British industry and commerce. Little attempt has been made to find a higher purpose for companies and even less effort has been put into trying to achieve employee commitment to the purpose. Occasionally when it is found, it is not only a vehicle for improving employee commitment and performance; it becomes a promotional opportunity as well. As outlined earlier, Jaguar suffered immense product quality problems in the seventies. John Egan's arrival as Chief Executive was followed by a purpose to achieve (again) quality pre-eminence – obviously a key factor in a quality car market. By employee involvement quality has been dramatically improved to the point that it's becoming a selling aid.

Jaguar is a good example of the results of the change process. Conventional thinking, if there is a quality problem, is to *add* product inspectors to contain the problem. However, if the employees can be committed, the errors at source can be reduced, people's commitment to their own work quality increased and the number of product inspectors *reduced*. A sure sign of basic commitment to quality is a plant with few inspectors. The reverse is equally true: armies of product inspectors always signify a lack of commitment by the employees involved in production. Put pride and purpose back into work and checks on products can be vastly reduced, yet how often is this the answer management strive for? In our industry rarely; poor quality is responded to by the traditional inspector's role being increased, thereby reducing people's responsibility in the process, not increasing it.

Many companies choose a purpose described by financial performance: return on equity of x or profit growth of y. Such yardsticks may be objectives but they are never a purpose or mission. A mission is usually qualitative (the *best* . . .) rather than quantitative (a return on equity of x). Equally a mission is rarely describable by financial performance – the financial performance follows from the mission being successful, it can not be the mission itself. Further, financial performance is not a goal which excites people or causes them to give of their best; this can only be achieved by stating 'why', not just 'what'. For example, a company may be faced with severe competition from an imported product. If the company's 'mission' is to reduce its unit costs by 30 per cent, this is unlikely to motivate anyone. However, if the mission is to 'beat the importer' this becomes an obvious goal with meaning which, properly communicated, will drive people to perform. The net result may well be a 30 per cent cost reduction but what an improved statement of intent to feel part of the battle to 'beat the competition' than be a contributer to a cost reduction!

So the first need is a purpose to which employees can align. If that purpose can't be stated, described and supported by management, then the company will be aimless and commitment will be low, and people will seek external purpose to their lives to make up for the lack of purpose in work.

When the purpose or mission is formed, the values the company wishes to operate within can be easily described. After expressing the mission, ask the question 'how?' and values will promptly follow, particularly if the question 'why?' is also addressed. The exercise must be carried out by the leadership of the organisation. Although later, in commitment it will be shared with middle management who can add their own dimension, the basic purpose and key values can only be set from the top. The leadership and his top management group would achieve this as described in the previous two chapters, working outside the work environment to agree the company's strategies, mission and the key values it will need to achieve success. By then identifying the priority areas, the list of values will become more defined. This definition can be further increased by similar working groups of middle and lower management and eventually shop-floor workers to add their own thinking into the process. An example would be:

COMPANY – JOE'S TAXIS

Mission or:
purpose
To be the best taxi service in town so as to maximise company and employee growth and reward.

How:
The achievement of this purpose depends on employee commitment based on trust and responsibility.

Values:
1. We will manage openly and create an environment of open communication.

2. We will listen to all good ideas from any source, and we will encourage people to innovate.

3. We will delegate decisions as far down the organisation as possible.

4. We will reward achievement individually.

5. We expect everyone to set the highest personal standards in dealing with our customers.

6. We will strive never to let a customer down.

The mission and values will vary enormously company by company and the process of describing them may take many weeks. However, they are an expression of the care, purpose and methodology of a company, so time is necessary to have them correct before they are communicated to others, inside or outside the company. It is the mission and values that employees identify with; simple business return is *not* a purpose and inspires no one. Compare the achievement of a business return with Kennedy's famous challenge to NASA – to have a man on the moon by the end of the decade – which drove all men in a consuming purpose. Can you find the challenge of your business? If not, there is little chance of gaining people's commitment, even at senior levels. However, once a genuine binding purpose is shared by everyone in the company, revitalisation of performance can occur. Without purpose why should anyone stretch themselves to strive harder or strive for perfection? No one will.

7

COMMITMENT

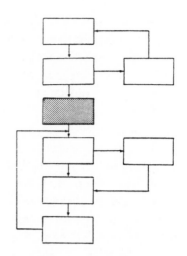

The first overriding commitment is that of the leadership, followed by that of the management to the company, its purpose and values. This process of change is so transparent compared with traditional British management's feudal style that top management's commitment has to be visible and real, and constantly be reinforced. Anyone without true identification will be seen through very rapidly and will distort the purpose and effectiveness of the organisation.

As will be seen later, the continuous reflection of purpose and values is an essential. This will be easy if it is genuinely felt but virtually impossible for those 'acting' the part.

The expression of commitment starts at the top: not asking of others what you would not do yourself. At the higher levels it is often a process of recommitment to the company, sometimes in preference to personal career progression, whilst at lower levels it is a process of commitment to the company above the external commitments to unions or other organisations. This does not necessarily mean a denial of trade unions, any more than a denial of a personal career. However, it does mean substituting the company purpose as the prime driving force.

It would be unreasonable to expect these changes lower in the organisation without top management personally and openly setting the example. Perhaps the massive earnings increases of many UK boards in the boom of 1984/85 have had a serious demotivating impact within many companies; the sadder fact is that this impact was not even discussed. Many people will accept bonus payments linked to company performance but it is hard to defend that only a small number of senior executives can share in the success of a company, particularly when in poor times they generally do not suffer the equivalent pain! Far better surely for everyone to share in the success – even if it be in proportion to basic pay.

How to start achieving commitment at the senior levels in a company has been previously outlined – by stating and agreeing the strategic mission and values. When this platform is established the process can be cascaded, by example, down the organisation. But without total senior management commitment it is difficult and often destructive to open up the process down the organisation. In many effective change processes up to 25 per cent of the leaders/ managers involved may have to be moved out of the line as they are unable to generate the degree of commitment required or their beliefs and practices are so firmly fixed in the old methods that they find it impossible to change life-time habits and patterns of work. However, it is essential to remove this core from line responsibility, otherwise too much energy will be used up in accommodating their inconsistencies and rationalising their differences.

All this is an example of how the seven change elements fit together. *Commitment* at higher levels has to be visible and *consistent*. One uncommitted manager can become a beacon for people to move towards and he will certainly become a reference point for those wishing to negate the overall process. Indeed, in this role he may well assume an importance beyond his normal role. This is not to say every senior less committed person should be fired but such persons should certainly be moved from a position of supervision where they can directly influence behaviour by suggesting work standards or practices different from those required in the 'new' environment.

How to achieve commitment has been covered earlier; the sharing of purpose and the generation of priorities is one very powerful mechanism at senior levels. This same process can then be cascaded right down a company. At lower levels the question to ask is 'what does the mission mean to *our* group?' – 'what are *our* priorities to achieve success?' Commitment comes from involvement, and this approach brings early involvement by asking rather than telling those involved.

So *commitment* must be universal at the higher levels in the company – and eventually at lower levels too. The easy option of ignoring the uncommitted is too harmful to the overall environment; this is most important at the more senior levels. The key issue is that commitment must be totally obvious to others because this type of change programme is a very transparent process. As we shall see next, *consistency* is another key element.

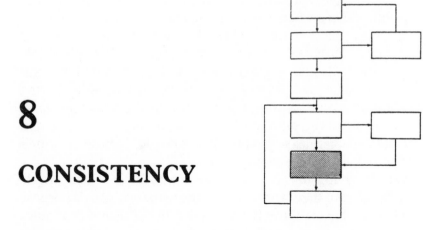

8

CONSISTENCY

There are four simple techniques for building consistency:

- **A** *Setting the Example*
- **B** *Envelope Management*
- **C** *Flags*
- **D** *Walking About*

Let's look at each in turn.

At home or socially we all act naturally, yet when we come to work we often change and become unnatural, acting in artificial ways. We shall see examples of this later, but consistency is much easier to achieve if it is natural rather than forced and therefore it is often worth asking 'what do I do differently at work than at home?' If there are differences, the right way will be to bring your natural home behaviour into work; try it the other way around for a day and you will soon be told what is wrong!

A. *Setting the example*

Setting the example is the first of the four techniques for building consistency and the home comparison holds up well. At home we raise our children by example. We might well use many methods to discipline, correct or guide our children but at the end of the day, the example is probably the most powerful. This is particularly true into teenage when other methods become harder to apply!

It is as true at work – whatever the communications in a company or its disciplinary procedures – that leading by example is a key method of achieving consistency. This will entail the tight control of values and progress towards the mission whilst having or allowing looser control of people within the tight boundary. Strive to show the *purpose* of the company and how it should operate and then leave people alone to make their own contribution. *Lead more and manage less.*

We are trying to develop the environment in which people willingly give of their best to contribute to the company's purpose or mission. This requires the leadership to define and communicate that purpose, as we have already seen, and then to set the example in terms of how best to operate at work.

People work for people, not for organisations. We are all influenced by what our boss feels, projects to be, or says is important. For example, if he never dwells on safety then we will tend to downgrade its importance ourselves. If working conditions are never mentioned, it is likely we will not be on the look-out in this area either. So consistency is achieved by always projecting the same important areas and these must include the purpose and the goals of the company. If this is naturally felt it is easy, if it is not it will be hard work; hence the need for commitment to be real.

Leadership, as will be discussed later, is about just that: *leading* others and setting the example in behaviour and what is important – just as we all try to do at home.

B. *Envelope Management*

One method of opening up consistency is *envelope management.* This requires you to look at your job and see how much of it can be carried out by those reporting to you. Each of us overlaps those under us and this often reduces the effectiveness of others in the process. This can occur in two ways: *physically* doing work that should be, and is capable of being, carried out by others and *checking* the work of others which effectively reduces the responsibility of their work.

46

How many managers check their secretary's typing? In British industry I would expect nearly 100 per cent. Yet every time you check you reduce the secretary's responsibility. She (or he) is paid to type accurately – you are not – and by checking, a safety net is being provided below the secretary's work. The secretary will be subconsciously aware of the checking process and so will be *more* likely to make mistakes. However, the knowledge that work is *never* checked not only increases accuracy, it increases job responsibility. It also releases your time and makes your own function more effective. A powerful multi-edged sword: work quality is improved, work authority is delegated and self-efficiency is increased.

A more insidious mechanism, often seen in larger companies, is the checking, in a negative sense, of others' work. How many letters/presentations/memos are written by others and signed by you? Give back work responsibility to the worker – it will generate enthusiasm and efficiency. If the subject warrants your approval, add a cover note saying you support the work carried out by the person responsible. Why take away the thrill of achievement from other workers? How many presentations. etc., have to be previewed by a boss before being given to *management*, where the subordinates' involvement and work is often not recognised.

To achieve envelope management, critically review your job for:

- What can be given to those below you?
- How can I eliminate duplicated checking? If I have to continue it, at least let me publicly recognise the originator.
- What meetings do I run? What is their purpose and are they necessary?
- What level of detail do I expect others to have and do I myself require?
- What do I represent to others in work? Do I exhibit 'proxy management' – that is, the apparent ownership of others' work?

When your list of give-aways is assembled, give them away publicly. You will be left with the key parameters of your job which are significant and important for you – an envelope of your responsibility – and the rest will be cascaded away from you.

For example, if manpower cost is significant to your job, you may be receiving regular data on wage rates, overtime, absence, etc. People working for you probably feel little direct responsibility for these areas because they know you check and monitor each. But what if you just received *total* manpower costs and then, by exception if there was a problem with the total cost, asked for an explanation of the other factors. Staff would feel an identity and responsibility for *their* own areas rather than feel it is *your* responsibility. Your envelope is total cost. Yet if you always receive the detail, you are receiving data which in the main is the responsibility of others to control. By receiving it you are diluting their authority and could well be diluting real control: whose problem is it, theirs or yours? If you receive all the data you have all the accountability, otherwise there's no purpose, except self-interest, in receiving the data. By changing, you divest the accountability whilst retaining overall control.

Perhaps you receive the data to be in a position to answer questions from above, i.e. the standards of detail are being set by those above you. Here is the consistency check. If you are in such a position and are asked a question of detail you have to be able to say, 'I don't know but if you feel it important I'll get the data for you'. This will probably have the result of removing the question! Yet we all often feel it is impossible to say 'I don't know'. When it's not heard, it is a sure sign the organisation is clogged with detail at every level, as each person keeps prepared to answer *any* question from above. Break the chain, the effect is dramatic and the time released enormous.

Act as you do at home: you don't read your daily paper cover to cover, every article. You filter and read the important and relevant parts only, yet at work you are often perceived to read the whole paper. This forces the next level down to be similarly armed with data just in case the question is raised. The whole company clogs up. One unfortunate impact of computerised data bases has been to worsen this process; the Board may receive ten times the data they can use. If data does not cause action its purpose is trivial – in fact, it can only be for 'checking', the destructive process that belittles others.

You may check your spouse's housekeeping; however, you don't find it necessary to check on all the purchases – just try doing so for a while and see the demotivated reaction. Yet this is exactly what so many of us are perceived to do at work.

The envelope technique releases time, generates trust and responsibility and raises work standards. It is a key element of consistency and a strong empowering process. As trust develops, other features of apparent control which actually are ineffective can be removed.

Clocking on and off, for example, is a belittling and ineffective process. Your interest is in getting achievement in work and raising standards, yet so often the day is started and finished like a school room, saying 'I don't trust you to arrive at work on time or give me a full day's work so I'll make you clock in and out'. What happens? The man arrives on time and then wastes time before he begins work or he queues to clock off! How many time clocks have you seen without queues developing before clocking-off time? And it's not just hourly paid people; staff on flexitime have been known to achieve the last half minute by pressing a lift button, waiting for it to arrive, *then* clocking off to 'earn' the small time that the lift takes to arrive. Impossible? Just check your own situation, it may well be happening.

These features are not a problem of the staff's attitude; it's management's for having created an environment where it is acceptable. It is an open statement of lack of commitment, which will be a reflection of the leadership's own perceived commitment.

The principle of envelope management is to shed work and responsibility down an organisation to its most effective level. An analogy is having a bet on a horse-race. Decide what you would comfortably wager, say £5. If you win you would be *pleased*. However, if you gave the £5 to your teenage child and he wagered and won, he would be *excited*. Similarly, at work, giving away parts of your job that you might even feel are *mundane*, for the next level down may well feel *exciting* because of the increase in responsibility and satisfaction.

This technique therefore improves commitment as involvement is increased, and it also shows consistency in the value of giving trust and delegating to the lowest level in the company where work can be effectively performed.

C. *Flags*

Another early and effective way of demonstrating commitment is to seek out 'flags'. These are things that are important *to those below* in your behaviour as signals of your commitment to the values and purpose you are trying to follow and establish. They are keys to achieving commitment through your consistency.

An easy way to define the list is to gather a group of first-line supervision together and *ask* them to list the things management do which are inconsistent with the purpose and values of the company. They will list scores of them, and you can then categorise them into those that are most significant – the real flags – and tackle them.

Examples will be: hours of work of management, time of arrival, length of lunches, privileged car-park spaces, etc. These are the devisive elements of your company, which if you are out to achieve total binding commitment will have to be removed. They propagate 'us and them' when you are driving for 'we'. Why should the M.D. have a reserved car space next to the door so he can remain dry while everyone else gets wet? What does that say to everyone else? Do you want to say this to everyone else? Are you aware of the effect of this privilege on everyone's attitude? Now is it *really* so important that the M.D. keeps dry, or is the attitude effect of the perk too big to ignore?

Why not fill the car park on a first-come first-served basis, as happens outside work, whether it be a football match or a British Rail car park? This might well encourage managers to start at the same time as shop-floor workers, which would itself be a large step forward in consistency and would help make 'us and them' turn into just 'us'.

Better to eliminate these flags of inconsistency: you will be involving others, you will be openly demonstrating your commitment and the visibility will begin to affect others.

D. *Walking About*

Finally, check the impact as you tackle flags and delegate trust through envelope management by *walking about*. You'll be releasing your time at a rapid rate; use the space to check the process.

Demonstrate your interest and care by talking to people in their work environment. You can't see from afar. Politicians plead this regularly and fail to make themselves believable. A manager is just that: looking after people, and to achieve that at least 25 per cent of *any* manager's job can only be discharged by visiting those he manages.

Besides showing interest in people, ask questions to check the environment and views of others. Is information getting down through the organisation (see Chapter 9)? Are opinions being heard and represented properly? Use your own ears and eyes to sense whether the environment and attitudes you are seeking are being shown in the different areas of your company or your work area.

Finally, in all these processes remember the lowest-level supervisor: the first-line supervisor. He, to his people, is management and represents the company. We shall see later how important it is to equip him for his role, and it is equally important here. Space has to be given for this job to be seen to have authority; so often the first-line supervisor is squeezed into a box of little authority. The natural result of cascading delegation down the organisation should be to give this specific job – the last in the supervising chain – a lot more scope and visible responsibility. As this position is a pivot for change everything you can to do to enhance it will be of significant value to the whole change process. Without the commitment of this level any programme will be severely limited.

Commitment and consistency are twins and the process can be summarised as follows:

- The process is *transparent*.
- Top management *must show commitment*.

Set the example – in words, ways and actions.
Envelope management – open up trust, delegation and job responsibility.
Use flags – visible signs for others.
            not necessarily the important issues but the visible inconsistencies.

Walk about yourself.
Reach the entire management chain – remember the lowest supervisor is
management to those below him.

- Envelope management

Move controls back to key parameters only:

Check by walking about.
Creates space.
Creates time.
Increases delegation and trust.
Increases involvement.
Taps people's potential to contribute fully.
Fosters self-responsibility.

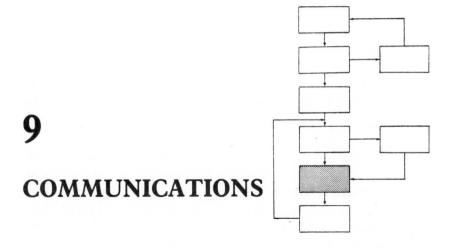

9

COMMUNICATIONS

Most managers'training for *the* key part of their job – communicating – is limited at best and zero at worst: happy amateurs in an environment which increasingly demands professionalism. Companies today often prepare senior executives for television or radio appearances – a rare requirement for the average manager – yet blissfully ignore the training of the same individual to discharge his responsibilities to communicate within the company, the part of the work he is primarily paid to perform.

The days of 'mushroom' communications – keep everyone in the dark and occasionally apply a dose of 'bull' – have gone forever. If people's discretionary potential is to be released, we have already seen this can be achieved only by informing them of the company's goals and purpose, aligning them to it, and feeding back results and progress. How is this to be done without a professional approach? The same companies who ignore this skill at their peril would not dream of operating their machinery in an unprofessional way. The machines are managed more professionally than the work force, yet *managers* even by title are named to indicate their prime purpose.

Before discussing how to achieve effective communications let us first see why communications, even of simple matters, often break down.

Why Communications Fail

1. *Thirty per cent retained.* An individual's capacity to remember a presentation or communication is naturally about 30 per cent. That means two thirds of all that is said is forgotten. Easy to understand why we misunderstand; we can effectively retain little or only parts of a message.

2. *Filtration.* Because our capacity to retain messages is poor we naturally appear to filter much information we are given. This process is apparent when a company item is communicated *down* the line; it equally happens when we receive feedback from the workforce to be transmitted *up* the company. Besides this form of filtration, we all also filter for personal, often subconscious, reasons. If the message to be given is difficult, we might dilute it to make it easier; if it is embarrassing we'll make it less so. For example, in the appraisal of your people you will remember how easy it was to be totally honest with the good performer compared to the poor performer. Similarly, on feedback, if those reporting to a manager have grievances or views that the manager feels may reflect poorly on his own perceived performance, he may well filter them out entirely or dilute them when passing them on.

By these mechanisms, clear information up and down a company's structure may rapidly become distorted and diluted. The workforce's understanding of the company is eroded and management's ability to 'read' its workforce becomes increasingly difficult. Misunderstanding grows, understanding declines.

3. *Decisions are communicated, but not the information on which they were based.* It is far easier to understand and agree with decisions when you have an appreciation of how they were made, what information was available and how was it used. Imagine at home just informing the family of a decision with no rationalisation of that decision; you would have many difficulties if this was your style. Yet at work this often is our normal style. How strange that in our own environment we naturally succeed, yet at work we unnaturally fail to rationalise our decisions and then wonder why we fail 'to get through'. As we shall see later, we need to extend our natural home behaviour into work – a recurring

theme in turning ineffective behaviour at work into the effective methods we use at home or socially.

4. *Non-specific communications*. The most common example of non-specific communication is the company notice board. If an important piece of information *first* appears in the form of a notice, it is a sure sign that the company's communication system is poor. If the information is really significant, it will be important to the company to ensure everyone receives the information and understands it. This in turn means each manager or supervisor requires thorough briefing so that he can professionally inform his own work group – in the way most appropriate to them – allowing the opportunity for questions of clarification. As we shall see later, for example, it is always critical that supervisors acquire knowledge before shop stewards. The act of communicating properly reinforces that the item is important; it can always be followed up by a notice, as confirmation.

A simple notice, no matter how well written, can *never* communicate well and, just as significantly, there is no control with a notice in terms of the order that people are informed. It has the effect of a hand grenade exploding: it will hit some and miss others and the spread of information is arbitrary as is the order that people see it. It cannot achieve the *variety* of presentation that may be required to suit different people. The whole impact is uncontrolled.

Yet many companies use notice boards to announce complicated wage settlements, company results, redundancy programmes, major reorganisations and many such sensitive and important news. No wonder such items are often misunderstood and employee reaction so often so vigorous!

The classic reminder of this is the early 1980s British Rail advertising theme of 'This is the Age of the Train'. In some quarters – particularly the London suburban commuting areas – this theme was taken to be an explanation for the ancient rolling stock in use! Not quite the effect British Rail had in mind.

So it is not surprising that notice boards are ineffective as a communication medium. They have a role as a reminder point for people to reconfirm a message but they should *never* be used as the first communication point for anything of importance. If they are used for important items then the readership will be variable,

55

totally uncontrolled, the order that people read them in will be arbitrary, and as no discussion is possible the net effect will be an ineffective and misunderstood communication.

5. *Lower management supervision is left unprepared.* Managements of some companies complain that their first-line supervision lack authority and perhaps even identify with the workforce rather than the management! In the same companies you usually find that management has put no effort into treating supervision as part of management or into informing them properly.

For most of the workforce the only frequent daily contact with the company is the first-line supervisor. He is the company and he is certainly the representative of management. If a question is asked of the supervisor and he does not know the answer, it is a failure of management as well as the supervisor. It belittles the supervisor and the company, and the authority of both is undermined.

If a matter is important, take time to communicate it properly and this means the care and time to ensure supervisors understand clearly. In reality they probably have the vast majority of the employees under their charge, so they are *the* most important group to ensure they *know* the communication, *understand* it and are *briefed well enough* to answer questions on it.

If due time is not taken then, as we've seen already, the filtration process is so effective that by the time the information seeps down to the first-line supervisor it is probably redundant (in time) and it will certainly be distorted and filtered. Often the only course open to a supervisor when confronted with a question is 'They don't tell me'. Abdication is seen as identifying with the workforce – but what other choice has the company given the man?

6. *Feedback rare and ineffective.* Two-way communication is necessary for an effective environment; and we have already seen how hard it is to achieve good one-way (down) communication. Feedback is filtered naturally – even more finely than downwards communication (see 2 above). If management does not take positive steps to gather and listen to feedback and people's opinions, it is unlikely that the feedback will even be offered after a short time.

Closed doors and management who never walk about or gather

informal unstructured opinions, are clear signs of blocked upward feedback. Even if gathering systems exist but no action is ever taken following views, opinions and ideas heard, then feedback will be choked off and cease. The responsibility of the listener is to show he has heard and, where appropriate, has done something. If the idea is not appropriate, say so and the line will stay open. Leave the donor in a vacuum and the line will close. Little wonder that in such environments the downward process will choke also; after all, why should those at the bottom of an organisation respond to management if management do not respond to the workforce? It has to be two-way and be demonstrated to be so. Again take the analogy in the home: if feedback is not listened to and responded to there, it will soon create significant problems.

7. *Accountability is low.* We have seen that communicating is one of the key roles of any manager, yet in how many companies is this part of a manager's job actually measured? We all respond to what we feel or what we are told is important. If some emphasis in appraisals is not concentrated on this area, the company by omission is implying that it is not important. However, when the communication performance is emphasised – both in terms of downwards communication and feedback acquisition – the response is immediate. Tell people what is required and they will perform; ignore this area and it will be ignored.

8. *Inconsistency.* Communications are complex and made up of:

- What is said
- What is done
- What is not said
- What is not done
- What is written
- What is not written
- How people act
- What is 'felt'

Even when companies concentrate on communications, all too often their concentration is only on the written word. Company magazines are checked and double-checked for non-political (in a company sense) presentation – items must not give away real information. Very often company literature which started as a genuine attempt at improving knowledge ends up diluted. So the average chairman's annual message is a collection of good news and self-congratulatory statements. The company newspaper is non-specific and filled with births, deaths, anniversaries and marriages! Notices are similarly vetted and very often need an authority level for review well above that which is sensible.

Even in an environment of professional written communication, messages will be disbelieved if management's actions are inconsistent with the message. That inconsistency can appear in the other styles of communicating – what is done/not done, how things are done, what people feel. A simple inconsistency is for the company to have a prime value which is never endorsed and re-emphasised by managers in their daily work. If timeliness is a requirement yet the manager himself arrives late or takes long lunches he will never be able to have people willingly – or probably even unwillingly – adhere to higher standards than he himself sets. He is saying one thing but his actions, which people will perceive as the *real* message, say something else. One company wished to create a value of team spirit and achievement in their people, yet out of work, in the street, the directors rarely acknowledged their presence, nor in work ventured out from their offices to invite informal contact. The actions spoke louder than the words, and staff's cynicism grew as they saw the inconsistency in this one area and presumed the same double standards in other areas of the company.

Inconsistency is one of the greatest threats to a company, and as we have seen already consistent projection and action is a must to achieve a sense of purpose in all employees.

9. *Information is power*. Sadly the recognition of this simple fact is often lacking in industry. Indeed, the extreme is when management tells union representatives of changes before telling supervision or lower management. As we saw earlier, nothing will undermine a supervisor faster than his people learning from a shop steward before he knows himself. All new information must reach

supervision before it is learnt from any other route. Abdication of this principle is the fastest possible way of belittling supervision, yet it occurs all the time. Why? Because strangely companies have come to have to respect and protect union representatives before their own supervision. In such organisations those stewards are being sustained and fed on the information diet just as the supervision is being starved. Reverse the process and not just the information but the *power* of information is given back to supervision – where it rightly belongs. In turn this builds authority and provides one of the key elements of leadership.

So if this list exemplifies why communications fail, what needs to be done? Let us examine each of the above features and see how to eliminate weakness and convert it into strength:

1 and 2. *Thirty per cent retained and filtration.* Firstly you may not believe the retention level is so low. Do a simple test to check this. Have someone read the statement below, ask the message to be passed verbally to someone else, then have that person repeat it to a third person (who was not listening to the first). Finally have the third person repeat it and compare this final version with the written statement. It will be totally distorted.

Message

You have just seen a road accident, please pass this description on to the police when they arrive:

'I was driving north at 30 mph, approaching a crossroads, following a red bus about 50 yards in front of me. A white Fiat sports car going south suddenly, without signalling, cut across in front of me. It appeared to cut the corner as it turned and hit a stationary Austin mini, which was waiting to come out of the side road. It had just started to rain.'

Try it: the loss of message content is enormous. Now imagine, as often happens, a real-life situation where a company passes a complex message down the line, perhaps on a sensitive industrial relations issue such as the state of a current wage claim. The message is often five times as long and contains nuance as well as fact. By the time it reaches level 3 or 4 or 5 down the organisation, *it has no chance of even representing the original message*. But this happens daily in some organisations!

What can be done? There are four key steps:

- 1. Simplify messages.
- 2. Write them down, if at all possible.
- 3. Repeat them.
- 4. Allow question time.

It's a time-consuming process to get communication right, but if the time is not taken so much damage can be done that it is probably less dangerous to say nothing. Yes really, fish get caught only when they open their mouths, and companies may well be safer saying nothing than destroying confidence by miscommunication.

Therefore, with important messages brief people in groups to allow questions and interpretation and issue a résumé for later use and memory assistance. Repeat the key points – if necessary several times. This may sound pointless, but you are decreasing filtration and increasing retention by so doing. Use the technique after a briefing of asking one of the audience to summarise the message to the group. This is a neat way of repeating and checking simultaneously; after all, it might be your description that is poor rather than the audience's absorption power!

3. *Decisions only are communicated.* By sharing *how* you arrived at a decision, as well as what the decision is, the understanding of that decision is increased. If a debate ensues it often moves the discussion from the decision itself to the data upon which it is based. This may sound devious but in fact ownership is the key which is so important when the person or group is in turn going to communicate to others. They understand the decision better and can rationalise it and if necessary defend it much better. They are more likely to say 'We decided that . . .' than 'He (or they) decided that . . .'.

Even difficult decisions are best shared. For example, if the company has to engage in a major personnel reduction, it is better to explain fully why and cascade this full knowledge down the line. It is also better to state the full scale of the impact rather than try to hide it – it will soon become obvious and without the full impact being known you will be adding uncertainty to the other stresses to be felt by the organisation. In one spectacular example in the early 1980s, a Canadian chemical company's redundancy programme was so ill-defined and misunderstood that an optimist was defined as anybody who took sandwiches for lunch! Perhaps a better course would have been an open statement of how large the cuts would be and where they would fall (and *why*); at least this way those unaffected would not have been so demoralised by uncertainty as to have had virtually the same stress as those eventually made redundant.

Obviously sharing the basis of decisions will not be necessary on every occasion, but for critical items with major impact in the company it is absolutely essential to build ownership. Decisions, particularly sensitive ones which cause difficulty, are nearly always those which are projected as They, the Management, the Company, i.e. when the ownership is felt to be very low. This feeling, caused by management not taking the necessary care and time to communicate properly, in turn leads supervision to divorce itself from the decision. Abdication by management and divorce by supervision – a recipe for disaster. Avoid this happening by taking the necessary time to share data and explaining *why* the decision has been taken as well as what the decision is to be. The ownership increase throughout the levels of supervision in the company will be dramatic and probability of effective action much increased.

4. *Non-specific communications.* Most audiences vary sufficiently in receptiveness to require individual treatment. Newspapers recognise this and people read the type they feel easiest with – for some *The Times*, for some the *Sun*. Similarly in communicating, it is unlikely that a standardised message will suit all people. Notices are non-specific: one message for all. If the message is important, the last place you should find it is on a notice board; it will have required individual group tailoring to be effective at all levels. The lazy way to communicate is through notices, and I have seen some incredibly important messages tossed out on notice boards; serious business results, short-time working, changes in hours, sensitive personnel changes. Even if a notice is to be used, it

should never be a surprise or shock and supervision should be prewarned and prearmed with supporting data before it appears – otherwise, as in Section 3 above, divorce will occur immediately. What other choice do people have but to disassociate themselves from the decision or the notice if they have no data to support it and, worse, they did not even know about it even one minute before those reporting to them!

So avoid non-audience communication. If it is important, do it properly and reserve the notice board for statutory notices and notices of promotion or change in which the display can add to an individual's (or group's) pride. It is an excellent medium for saying thank you for example; as we shall see, an event that occurs far too rarely in British industry.

5. *Lower management/supervision is unprepared.* Three simple rules:

- Ensure they receive information down the line before hearing it from other sources.
- Allow proper time for briefing.
- Write down information when possible.

The first rule is the key: never undermine supervision by exposing them to the problem of their people (or worse their shop stewards) hearing information first. In important communications it is worthwhile to write down the information, so as to reduce filtration and increase retention, and then also allow time for briefing so that questions can be asked to ensure supervision feels able adequately to represent the company.

6 and 7. *Feedback and accountability low.* The discipline of communicating has to be installed so that it becomes second nature to everyone. The easiest way to achieve this is:

- Set up scheduled information sessions in the line.
- Set up feedback sessions with management.
- Check information by walking about.
- Ensure communication is a key element in each manager's/supervisor's performance appraisal.

An example of establishing a second-nature system is to establish a weekly communications session in each business or functional area. It need not be long (maximum half an hour) and will probably fit into an existing meeting schedule. This period is reserved for the senior management to explain performance, plans, issues, etc., and for lower management to recycle feedback from the workforce. Besides general feedback, each month a specific question (or questions) upon which employees' views are sought can be given out to supervisors at such a meeting, with the requirement to present their people's feedback in a meeting perhaps in a month's time. The act of management adhering to this timetable will quickly make supervisors seek out opinions and be ready to provide the feedback.

Now having quickly established a gathering mechanism, it is critically important that management responds to that feedback. Lack of *visible* response will kill it very quickly. Therefore, senior management needs the same discipline – perhaps a short quarterly session – to listen to and decide action on employee feedback. Ensure each department manager knows he must present feedback either in general or on specific topics that have been sent 'down the line' as questions. Again very quickly your senior managers will realise feedback is expected; they will then ensure the mechanism works.

Finally, to ensure the entire workforce see results from the process, publicise actions, thank people for their input and above all do something in response to the feedback. If action is impossible or impractical then explain why because without explanation the inaction will be interpreted to mean management did not listen. Make sure this recycle is properly fed back down the line.

As two simple aids to the system, senior management on walkabouts should check that people have heard specific information items that you expected them to have heard, and ask for opinions on the process – open hearts as well as minds and ears! Ensure each appraisal of every manager and supervisor measures their performance in the area of communicating downwards and gathering and transmitting feedback.

Once such steps have been taken, the company is beginning to elevate communications out of the 'nice to do if you have time, but first to go if you have not' to 'essential to achieve our goals'. If it is seen to be important, real importance will be attached to the process and over time it will become second nature.

8. *Inconsistency*. This problem is corrected by example and a clear understanding of what is acceptable. If the leadership sets the example of a consistent open style, others will rapidly follow. When people deviate from the standards expected in this area, they have to be checked quickly. Remember the lowest supervisor can let the company down. He may be the only normal company contact to his people, so he effectively is the company. Therefore, his consistency of values must be as close to the leadership's as possible.

The process of change will take time and the catalyst is the leadership change and acceptance of consistency as a paramount need; others will follow the example once it has been carried through long enough not to be seen as a flash in the pan.

9. *Information is power*. This fact has been discussed under Section 5 above.

In summary, communicating is a time-consuming exercise. However, it is one of *the* key roles of management and without effective communications it is impossible to recharge an organisation and achieve high performance. The steps and features of effective communication are:

1. Keep it simple.
2. Write down as much as possible.
3. Repeat key themes often.
4. Explain why decisions are made.
5. Avoid notices: they are too audience non-specific.
6. Brief lower supervision thoroughly.
7. Never allow new information to come from other sources than down the line.
8. Set up regular communications (down) meetings.
9. Set up regular feedback meetings.
10. Put communicating in everyone's performance appraisal.
11. Don't allow inconsistency of values.

12. Lead by example.

13. Walk around to check progress and allow access.

Let us now in the next chapter look briefly at two methods of improving communication and gathering feedback – the audio-visual presentation and the opinion survey – and see a few other examples of helpful hints in the communication area.

10

COMMUNICATIONS: METHODS TO HELP THE PROCESS

Let us look at two techniques which may be used to help two-way information flow in a company. The **audio-visual medium** is a powerful tool for assisting upward as well as downward information flow; and the **opinion survey** is in growing usage to help determine views within a company.

Audio-Visual

Growing usage of this medium is occurring not only in training applications but also in communications. It is a powerful tool but to be fully effective requires some simple guidelines to be followed:

- Utilise it as *part* of the entire communications programme.
- Use simple common language.
- Brief those presenting the audio-visual.
- The subject presentation must be professional.
- Require follow-up action and debriefing.

Audio-visuals provide the opportunity to communicate directly to an entire workforce. However, this must be effected so as not to undermine or bypass management and supervision. It enables graphics and other visual-aid techniques to be employed to increase understanding and it often allows people to hear and see the message more than once, enabling retention to be increased. Audio-visuals can never replace normal communication channels; they are a supplementary aid only. In many companies they are the only visible effort put into communication (the annual results presentation or chairman's message, 'state of the nation', etc.) and in such cases they are often unprofessional, with those involved heaving a sign of relief when the exercise is over for another year.

However, they can be very effective as occasional complements to normal communications. Direct presentation by the leadership, who may be rarely seen in large organisations, is powerful as is the opportunity to transmit a common message to everyone free of all filtration and distortion. For full impact the recording needs to start and finish with an explanation of how this particular transmission fits into the overall company programme. Contexting the event is essential to prevent the flavour of a one-off exercise out of context with the rest of the company's activities.

In the preparation of the material to be used it is essential that the message is clear and that the language used is understandable to the recipients and free of jargon, buzz words or esoterics. The best way to achieve this is to write the script and then have it read and edited by a group of supervisors close enough to the shop floor to know the impact at this level. They can then remove the language which will be incomprehensible. Whenever possible utilise examples in the material that arise in work or use analogies from the home or sports to which people can readily identify.

But most important, keep it simple. If you are trying to reach everyone, talk and present it in a way that will be easiest to understand. If in doubt, always err on the side of simplicity. Even though you may feel you are being too basic it is often surprising how easily people are confused but, as we saw under feedback, those same people may be embarrassed to confess their misunderstanding.

Our attention span is limited, and any hope of large volume retention is lost if an audio-visual is over 15 minutes in length. Indeed, the most powerful messages are those contained in programmes of around eight minutes in length. Utilise the *visual* aspect as well as the spoken, by using graphics to relay key points and then overtalk these. Similarly, add to the familiarisation by using shots of the factory or office environment as much as possible.

The television medium is one seen frequently by everyone and it is a very professional presentation medium. If you are to have an audio-visual programme, it needs to be of an equivalent standard because the comparison is so obvious. You will often hear senior executives express concern about using the medium or being unwilling to take the time necessary to achieve public television standards of presentation. The advice is simple: if you can't achieve these standards do not use the medium. It requires the 'performer' to achieve the highest of standards, otherwise the viewer will be distracted from the message by the poor presentation itself. The body, the eyes, the hands, the voice, all must be in ordered control and professional. Also remember the transparency of the medium; if the presenter is uncommitted to what he is saying, it will rapidly become obvious.

Do not 'ad-lib'. The presentation must be free of 'umms' and 'aahs' and full concentration should be on the presentation without worrying about what to say next. Auto-cue must be used since a head bobbing up and down from paperwork notes is unacceptable. It is a serious presentation and *must* use all the professional aids available.

Many organisations exist to help produce such programmes and it is well worthwhile using their skills – at least for the first few programmes. Take their advice: wear clothes of colours (usually dark tones and blue shirts, for example) which are well balanced and use lighting to the standards of television. The presentation skills can be acquired quite quickly but time must be taken to achieve them. If the executive can not provide the time, the programme is not worth the effort and the attempt should not be made.

Very often the programme should be introduced by a member of staff, perhaps the supervisor or manager of the group involved. *Never* allow an audio-visual to be shown without this control. Lunch-time unattended showing or any unattended presentation completely undermines the message. You have gone to cost and time to prepare it so ensure it is properly presented. Brief the introducers with likely questions and answers, and explain the introduction you require. Also remind the introducer to ask for feedback on the programme so that you can have a learning experience to amend future attempts if necessary. This debriefing is most important to ensure that the programme is live and important and seen to be so. Indeed, action resulting from the feedback to prove the point is as important as it is in opinion surveys. If you just receive feedback and no visible action results, feedback will quickly dry up.

With attention to these brief guidelines, audio-visuals can play a very significant part in any communications programme. However, it is a very professional medium so *you must attain the standards of the profession.*

Audio-visuals can also be used to communicate *upwards*. In this case the professional aspects need not be adhered to in the same way. The importance now is the content, not the presentation. Nevertheless, audio-visuals can be as powerfully used upwards as downwards and people find it a 'fun' medium. It can be a very effective form of group presentation.

Opinion Surveys

As the communication flow in an organisation improves, natural in-line information will readily move up and down the organisation. But opinion surveys – either on specific or general topics – are an excellent way of showing openness and providing a barometer of views. If they are used, they can also provide a way of positively measuring attitude, an area that is otherwise difficult to gauge. 'How is morale? – Good!' is one test, but it is hard to judge progress in this way! Periodic opinion surveys will provide an ability to measure attitude and its change over an extended period, and like all other aspects of life it is rewarding to measure progress rather than just assume it.

To kick a survey off, it is worthwhile the leader explaining to everyone why he wants to carry out a survey, why it is important, and what he would like to discover. This is best achieved by bringing management and supervision together to explain to them first, so they in turn will be able to handle questions lower in the organisation. This step is necessary as described previously: make sure supervisors are placed to be a knowing part of the exercise so as to keep it an 'our exercise' rather than 'theirs'.

Following this first step, a letter with the opinion survey can then be sent to those involved. How trade union representatives are handled is peculiar to the structure in each company; however, it may well be worth assembling stewards and union representatives and explaining to them the purpose and importance of the survey. This should occur *after* the supervisory briefing session to ensure stewards do not have information before supervisors, which would otherwise subvert the supervision.

Two final key steps before launching the survey: first, be committed to summarising the survey results and *acting* on them and, secondly, as under audio-visuals, although you select the areas of questions, do allow supervision to review them to ensure they are clear to the recipients.

Allow the questionnaire to be completed in work-time. Although many will be completed out of work, if the exercise is important to you, allowing time in work will demonstrate the importance to others. Do not be over-optimistic on the time required to complete the questions. Ask for replies in about six weeks – this will capture those sick, absent on holidays, etc., and will also allow a reminder on completion to be sent out towards the end of the time period.

Ask for the returns to be sent to the leader requesting the survey. This personalises the questionnaire and again raises the importance of the event.

The questions themselves should be posed so that accommodation of data is convenient and meaningful. This is often best achieved by writing a series of statements and inviting the recipients to show scaled agreement/disagreement. For example:

		1	2	3	4	5
1.	I am clear on the Company's goals.	☐	☐	☐	☐	☐
2.	I am clear on my own work group's goals.	☐	☐	☐	☐	☐

3. I am well informed on the Company's progress.

4. I often see my manager.

5. I have plenty of opportunity to discuss problems with my supervisor.

6. Management listen to my concerns.

Instructions: Tick one box to indicate your support for each statement, where

1 = Strongly agree	4 = Disagree
2 = Agree	5 = Strongly disagree
3 = No view/neutral	

The data, when summarised, will provide not only the average view but will also show strongly polarised opinion. This is particularly important as such pockets of opinion can be illuminating in terms of local problems, supervisory issues or areas of miscommunication/misunderstanding which require attention.

This leads to two final features of the questionnaire. First, invite recipients to give their name or at least their department and, secondly, allow space at the end of the questionnaire for comments, either on the format of the survey or any other points the recipient would like to raise. If the points arise as questions (of policy or data), ensure answers are given after the survey, either in a general feedback or specifically to the questioner. This recycle strongly reinforces the importance of the survey and of the questions raised. If on the first survey many people receive direct answers to questions or comments, you may guarantee the next survey will have an even higher response and you will rapidly break down the historical reticence to surface and air views.

Following a survey, it is mandatory to feed back the results to the company personnel. This can be achieved through the line, by direct communication from the leader (written or audio-visual) or a combination of methods best suiting each organisation. However, the feedback should be meaningful and have the following features:

- General comments by survey area (communications, business results, etc.).
- Specific areas of success or concern – and in the latter case the management's plan on how these concerns will be followed up.
- Direct action commitment. It is essential, as a result of the survey, that management commits to and completes some meaningful follow-up action. This powerfully reinforces the exercise. It helps future surveys and makes the exercise worthwhile and be seen to be so.

The level of survey return is a key indicator of openness and attitude in an organisation. A better than 80 per cent return is excellent; below 50 per cent indicates problems of attitude, both in management and workforce, exist. It is common for the first survey to be low in return but when follow-up action is seen, subsequent surveys rapidly climb up to the 80 per cent plus level.

In summary, the opinion survey, when properly carried out, is a powerful tool for measuring attitude in an organisation, both across the company and for detecting polarised pockets of opinion within the company. It is a unique process for demonstrating action from management and thereby greatly aids the open flow of communication. Surveys also provide a real-time method of measuring progress, substituting hard data for 'feel' and thereby helping to reinforce (or otherwise!) that 'feel' in on-going issues. But like all other aspects of communication, carry out the surveys efficiently and effectively and demonstrate action after them.

11

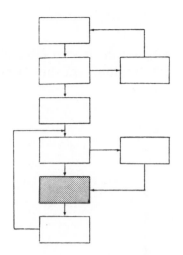

CULTURE

Culture can be defined as the behaviour of and in an organisation – its environment, its 'feel', what it represents to those within it. At the same time culture can be both the largest obstacle to change and the strongest catalyst for change. Let us first see how culture operates.

We have seen already that mission, purpose and values have great impact on an organisation and it is at this level that change processes often begin – by leadership restating the purposes of the organisation and how it will operate. Yet in 90 per cent of UK companies these simple descriptions of the organisation have never been made at all. However, even in these companies, people will *assume* them though they have never been written down or communicated. People's behaviour will indicate their values and their purpose, so in the absence of a positive description *observed behaviour will set values and purpose.*

The same is true for all features of culture: normal day-to-day events will set 'norms' which people automatically identify and respond to. Indeed, without leadership in *expressing* these values/ purposes, the usual problem in organisations is inconsistency between individuals who each interpret and behave as they think the organisation requires.

Let us see the three levels on which culture operates.

Levels of Culture

Edgar Schein very effectively described the levels of culture in organisations in his paper entitled 'Corporate Cultures' as follows:

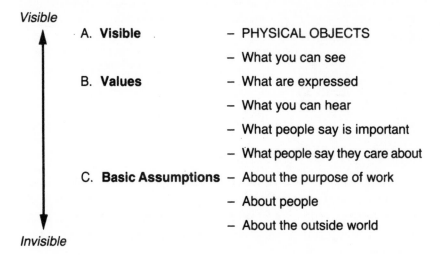

Visible

A. **Visible** — PHYSICAL OBJECTS

— What you can see

B. **Values** — What are expressed

— What you can hear

— What people say is important

— What people say they care about

C. **Basic Assumptions** — About the purpose of work

— About people

— About the outside world

Invisible

Let us see in more detail what these culture levels mean in an organisation.

1. *Visible level.* Culture is seen and felt through the physical objects in a company. Offices and workplaces shout out the visible culture. Are offices plush and lavish, how do they compare with workforce conditions? Do top management locate their offices remotely? The usual case is on top of the building protected by separate access and the warden-like skills of a powerful secretary. The management might say it wants open communications, yet its visible culture says it wants to remind people of rank and status and the open-door policy is effective only if you have the power of perseverance to arrive at the open door! On the shop floor, poor canteen or changing facilities say how much care the management project to others. Again, the words may be, 'we care equally for all', but if conditions are so much poorer on the shop floor, these will speak far louder and more effectively than the words.

The best two guides to the physical culture differences in a company are canteens and lavatories. Both express precisely the culture between levels. Directors with their own dining room and toilets, descending to often dirty canteens and toilets for hourly paid people scream out the social divisions in a company. Little chance of equality of organisation, pride and purpose in such companies. Indeed, the first culture change and the most effective in such places is probably to scrap the directors' dining room and toilets and clean up the workforces' facilities, or better still invest in totally common facilities.

How are places of work furnished? In many UK and US companies you can accurately estimate rank by visible privileges: pictures on walls, number of windows, carpets or not, and the presence of plants. I've known one company in which considerable organisational discomfort was created by a newly promoted individual refusing his 'badges' of rank.

Clothing – how do people dress? One group in overalls, the rest in suits is a good indicator of a divide. For some work this is obviously necessary; however, the formality of dress gives a good indication of the formality of structure too. Many overseas companies have unified dress to try to say 'we are all individuals and we respect each other'. In many boardrooms, even on sweltering days, jackets will be kept on as a defensive cultural gesture to maintain formality and the order of precedence and rank.

Notices – how are they structured? The formality and rank is often visible. When leaders write to employees, are letters addressed 'Dear Colleague' or 'To all Employees' – an excellent sign of whether it is 'us' or 'us and them'.

Office doors – open or shut? In most companies doors are shut and they are saying keep out, communications are fixed and formal and boxes are created. Go to most head office locations and you will find miles of corridors all with closed doors. People's interaction is low and the visible culture tells you so.

By walking around a work location you can quickly observe the visible signs of culture and equally quickly estimate the culture. It may not be the culture expressed by the leaders, but it is certainly the one seen and felt by the people in the company.

These few examples of visible culture are sufficient to illustrate the point: the physical running of an organisation is visible to all and sets the culture. So it is pointless the leadership expressing other wishes if the physical aspects deny these expressions. Here is the point in writing down values and purposes because by doing so and then walking around to check consistency, it will be easy to see what needs to be done to bring the physical aspects in line with the expressed wish. Without altering the physical it is unlikely the expressed wish will even be heard, let alone believed!

2. *Values level.* Values are a stage less obvious than the physical aspects of a company; they describe the things that people say are important or that they care about. We have covered some of the value impacts above because physical objects in a company spin off into values. However, this level itself is more concerned with what you can hear in a company – what people say themselves about the company and what seems to be important.

What are the most significant departments? This gives the first clue. Are sales seen above production in the hierarchy? Is customer service seen as very important? Relative department status – which always exists – gives a good guide to where the company is perceived to have significance or value. It is unlikely that customers are at the top of a company's values if the sales and customer service departments are low in the hierarchy, and this is often witnessed by the quality of personnel assigned to these departments. In many companies the customer service group is staffed with perceived (or even actual!) rejects – failed salesmen or individuals from other functions 'hidden' in this low-profile department. If this is the case, then it is no good the leadership expressing customer service as a key value; the organisation will perceive this not to be so.

Equally, is the board staffed with engineers, as is often the case in technology intensive companies? If so, people may well perceive a similar low valuation on selling or customer service skills.

Again, if production is a lowly perceived function then quality may often not be taken as seriously as the company requires. Quality is driven by the market; however, unless it is given emphasis inside the company the impact may not reach all levels of the organisation. Production may work to an overwhelming cost drive where quality can often cause conflict, and it needs structural importance to be perceived to achieve balance.

The 'folklore' of an organisation often provides a real guide to the 'feel' and values within. Remembered and quoted events themselves create the atmosphere of what people admire or feel important. Are the stories centred around major sales gains or around production events? The balance in a company is often described accurately by the repetition of these events.

Asking people what *they* feel is important tells you what values the organisation is expressing. The opinion survey is a useful mechanism for discovering this emphasis. Very often because the perceived stress area is different from that expressed by leadership, inconsistency in values becomes quickly apparent. In many industries management rightly puts personnel safety high on its priority list. Yet if meetings routinely never have safety on their agenda, or management rarely raises safety issues whilst walking about, then the workforce will not believe this concern. To promote a value, it needs consistent emphasis daily and weekly; most managements lack the consistency and professionalism to achieve this.

3. *Basic assumptions.* The third level of culture is the expressed purpose of the organisation: what it is trying to achieve, how it deals with its people and how it relates to the outside world. The purpose, as explained previously, answers the questions: why are we here? What is our ultimate goal? This may be expressed as a vision, a mission, a purpose, which is quite different to an objective. The mission is rather like a lofty beacon – visible from all corners of the organisation and often expressed as a guiding principle. Examples of company missions have been given in earlier chapters, and you will remember they invariably are expressed as becoming the best at some feature of unique importance to that company – customer service, quality, etc. Objectives and goals are usually short-term measures of the path to be taken to achieve the mission.

Very often companies express goals and objectives only in physical terms *unrelated* to the mission, e.g. a certain return level for the next year, a sales growth of *x* per cent, a production target of *y*, etc. The mission is unreinforced if there is no objective target in this area as well. People align behind purposeful directions – a return target, for example, will switch on very few people.

As we have already seen, a mission statement will have to include an expression on values – 'how we will achieve the mission' – and a reference to the outside environment. This last point helps people understand the relevance of the mission, *and it has to be relevant.* For example, it would have been totally misguided for Shannon Airport in Ireland to have a mission to improve its services for transatlantic airlines just before engine performance was increased to the point where refuelling stop-overs were no longer necessary. A mission more related to the external environment would have been to concentrate on local and European service provision because the extension of flying journey lengths was always going to make the stop-over airport redundant.

Similarly, lack of purpose related to the external world was a major aspect in the decline of the UK motorcycle industry. As we saw on p. 18, after the war it was a very strong industry with virtually total share of the UK market. When the small Japanese bikes first arrived, rather than compete head on (i.e. a mission to meet Japanese quality and manufacturing costs, which were the real threats to the domestic industry) the industry declined to compete and retreated to the larger bike market.

With a volume base established, the Japanese very soon started to compete in the larger markets too and the UK manufacturers were rapidly broken and driven into extinction. This happened because the external environment, the nature of the threat, was not recognised and therefore the companies involved did not change their mission to meet the new threats. The demise of a whole industry resulted. But if management had recognised the threat, informed their workforce of the risks involved, and redirected their companies who is to say the combined energy thereby harnessed would not have won the day and the UK would still have a motorcycle industry?

Unfortunately, since the war UK industry is littered with similar examples where companies failed to recognise the real world and its threats until too late. Even when the threat was belatedly recognised, energy went into restricting the threat rather than facing it head on, so that import tariffs and other such actions were proposed effectively to ignore the threat. These of course were only temporary expedients at best and would never have provided a solution. The steel, coal, automobile, television, video recorder, camera, watch and transistor markets all provide excellent examples of the same blind spots which eventually caused industrial disaster.

Now in the 1980s some companies have at last begun to realise the challenges from the environment, and by beginning to obtain alignment of their workforce behind a real mission have started to release enormous energies which are making them internationally competitive (for example, Jaguar, British Steel, parts of the former British Leyland). If the same activities had started twenty years ago then perhaps our industrial base would not have been so eroded. Obviously the political and social climate of the UK has to share part of the blame for this process; governments themselves have rarely demonstrated a similar external awareness of the changing pressure of the real world. They worked for short-term gain by either promoting import barriers to protect home industries or by telling people 'they never had it so good', thereby adding to the unreality of not having to meet technology and competitive changes from abroad. Common market entry and the 1970s oil crisis eventually forced home the reality, but too late for the salvation of many companies and jobs.

It can be argued at length whether governments, unions (many of whom even today perpetrate the blindness to competition and support the import barrier approach, ignoring the fact that we are the most trade-dependent nation in the world) or managements bear prime responsibility for our industrial demise. However, lack of vision, of purpose, related to the real world is certainly the prime cause and at the end of the day all three bear heavy responsibility. Perhaps the problem is that all three would deny it.

So inside companies the need for clear related purpose is paramount and in this forum, management has total responsibility. The mission has to be explainable and supported by its relevance. It then needs to be fed into and flowed down the organisation as the first step in achieving employee alignment and commitment. With this real purpose, most employees will respond.

We have seen how culture works at three basic levels; clearly to achieve irreversible change in performance, culture must be affected at all three levels. We have already covered how this might be achieved:

- A statement of company purpose and values.

- Management communicating to all levels these statements, constantly and consistently reinforcing them in what they say, act and do.

- Searching out the inconsistencies in today's behaviour and

81

methods to change them into line with the defined purpose
and values.

The statement (by the leader) of a compelling vision of the company's future to which people can align is the first step, together
with the values that will operate to achieve progress towards this
mission. Having explained, discussed and opened up these
features, the management must then closely and consistently
follow them. A period of 'proof' will be necessary to convince
others of the genuine intent and purpose both of the mission and
management's commitment.

It will be found that the task is laborious but, following the
techniques suggested earlier of using lower levels of supervision to
point out the inconsistencies and help remove them, an effective
and fast route for change will be found. The key point is that the
changes will have to occur at *all* levels of culture.

For example, if competitive achievement is the key to survival,
then things will require changing to reflect this; no good the chief
executive officer preaching the need for economies whilst his own
style and behaviour remain unaltered. So imagine in the Dunlop
example the impact of the chairman's 21 per cent rise during a
period when the company was under the severest of competitive
threats and fighting for its life. The stronger the need, the more
severe the action required. Perhaps changing the company Daim-
ler for a Mini is extreme but it would have immediate impact! If
the position is severe enough why not make this change? Only
culture prevents it happening. Perhaps the reasoning that a pres-
tige car is necessary does not bear close examination; is the
necessity in the eye of the chairman or in other's eyes? His turning
up to a sales meeting with a customer in a Mini might be thought
'gimmicky', but I guarantee it would have an effect, no matter
how small, on the discussions.

One of the most difficult areas to manage and lead is in the value
level of culture. The leadership is represented by middle management and supervision and much effort will be needed to ensure
their consistency. An effective way to achieve this is to examine
who is rewarded in the organisation. Whatever the values
required by the company, they must be the key elements of
performance to be rewarded – by pay, recognition or promotion.
From the simple recognition of 'thank you' right through to

promotion, management must reward those who support the vision and values. This can be a far more effective method than 'punishing' those who act and work out of line with the values. If a specific behaviour is felt to be very significant, include it in annual performance appraisals to ensure it is understood to be important and it will be seen to be of significance.

So one of the key features of effective culture change is to ensure you affect *all* three levels of culture – visible, values and assumptions – seeking out inconsistencies and setting the example by reinforcement of positive values each day. Whilst the culture in a company can present a large obstacle to change, it can also be used as a catalyst for change. To turn culture into this *positive* force simply requires that culture at all three levels is first recognised and then made consistent with the organisation's aims. The old adage of leadership by example reminds us of one remarkably strong mechanism in the process. Everyone in a company is affected by culture, which is why demonstrated change and improvement in this area can have such an immediate and catalytic effect on the entire change process.

12

CHALLENGE

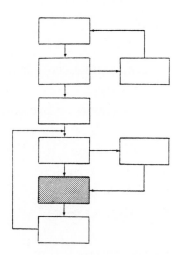

Whilst developing the first five C's – core mission, commitment, communications, consistency and culture – the effective challenging of the organisation is another very important catalyst to the entire activity. Much of this challenge will be initiated at the leadership level which brings into focus the aspects of effective leadership.

As we have seen, a requirement of the leader is to project the values and act in accordance with them throughout the working day, as well as constantly reinforcing the mission of the organisation. Unfortunately, many of today's leaders are so concerned with managing rather than leading that they fail to provide the impetus that will inspire the organisation to grow as individuals and collectively. Let us look at the behaviour difference between a leader and a manager in a leadership position:

The leader	*The manager in a leader's position*
• Talks about philosophy	• Solves daily problems, makes decisions
• Makes contact with employees at all levels	• Meets formally with subordinates
• Acts warm and supportive	• Acts aloof, critical
• Projects key values	• Inconsistent

The leader	*The manager in a leader's position*
• Concentrates on business strengths	• Concentrates on weaknesses
• Talks about future goals	• Talks about current events
• Does not plan to fill his diary	• Fills his diary
• Easy to meet	• Difficult to meet
• Integrates new people	• Rarely deliberately meets new people
• Anticipates future changes	• Little anticipation
• Uses intuition and thinks strategically	• Does not trust intuition

The challenge in an organisation is twofold: it is the leader and management challenging the organisation to change and grow and simultaneously it will be the employees challenging the leader's beliefs and values for their strength, sense and purpose. This second challenge will require time to pass before others begin to change themselves; confidence will have to be given and sustained that the new values and goals are worth following and this is why leadership strength and style is so important.

The leader's style is of the highest significance; it will be mirrored throughout the organisation over time; what he shows to be important will grow in importance. In the change process, as we have already seen, systems as well as people will require change to reflect new priorities. For example, it will be less easy to have a common system across business segments which are in different stages of development. As Chapter 3 showed, a new business cannot be led and measured in the same way as a mature business – the key parameters are totally different. Yet how many large companies have uniform accounting and key measurement systems, irrespective of the individual business development stages? Manpower counting is often the easiest to spot. A common counting and, more important, decision path process will exist for all business sub-segments. This completely ignores the need to grow the business at its innovation stage compared with the tightly monitored requirements of a mature business. However, leadership's inability to allow different systems will often stunt the growth of the developing business, either directly or more often indirectly where the management of the sub-unit will perceive the leader's style and needs and will limit the business through this implied pressure. Many multinationals cannot foster specialty business for this reason. They will recognise their inability but will seek 'entrepreneurship' instead and bemoan the lack of spirit in their companies. But how can the entrepreneur flourish if the company's systems are geared to achieving medians, norms and performance indices that are unrelated, by definition, to the needs of the entrepreneur's business?

For example, it is quite common for companies to check and compare (between units) their manpower by indices:

- Sales volume or value per salesman.
- Production volume per operator.
- Invoices handled per accounting head, etc.

However, in a growing specialty business, unit volumes may be very low but added value very high, whilst conversely in a mature 'commodity' business volume is large but added value small. On an index of sales per salesman the specialty business is very poor but on added value per salesman very high. The commodity business is obviously the opposite. But if the indices themselves are gospel because of the need to have a common cross-company system, the specialty business manager may be forced to *reduce* his salesmen just when his business needs increased selling activity. This happens in many large companies.

Another area to suffer quickly under common counting systems is the important area of customer service. Hard to quantify the benefits, but in an increasingly competitive world service is becoming a key differentiation between suppliers. In our standard counting world, this area is likely to suffer in numbers and as we have seen it already suffers in quality, often having been a 'dumping ground' for the less able employees.

So although we are concentrating on the leader himself – his style and behaviour – the company's systems also need to reflect the new values and priorities. Indeed, every system will need review; any system good for the 1960s is unlikely to be good or relevant enough for the 1990s. Yet again most organisations have their systems set in concrete. How to raise investment proposals, and measure their worth, remain unchanged from the days when supply dominated the world – growth was so certain and continuous that supply chased it continually. But today's world is of restricted growth with oversupply capacity, and so the market description and understanding is far more significant than the manufacturing issues. Yet this changed emphasis is rarely seen.

How people's performance is measured or their career planned provide other good examples. Appraisal forms are often unaltered, reflecting the priorities of the past, as is the process of career planning. In the 1980s and 1990s the equilibrium is shifting in the employer-employee relationship so that people require more say in their own development, but many appraisal forms have little space for this involvement. Companies still believe the old days of secrecy over plans, based on the company knowing all and knowing best, is preservable. But it clearly is not, and it is not in the company's or the individual's interest to be preserved.

Examination of company systems will reveal many such examples, unquestioned through the passage of a quarter of a century. Accounting and information also reveal much about the process in a company. What is regularly measured and who receives the data are key indicators. With the need for wider communication, how much of the company's accounting is spread through the organisation; even whether sufficient data is available for groups to discharge their activities is a real issue. Many companies are still restrictive, keeping profitability or even cost performance at very senior levels and thereby preventing people being able to see and measure their own contribution. Adequate for the 1960s, inadequate for the 1990s. Part of leadership's role is to examine critically the new needs generated by the company's mission and its values and then to revise and revitalise the corporate systems to align them to the new needs.

A useful checklist for the changes possibly required is to look at the corporate systems and carry out a searching review. The following list shows some fruitful areas for starting this examintion (how detailed the list needs to be is very much company-specific):

- Old principles   – Meetings, investment, appraisals
- Standard events   – Reviews, who needs data, accounting
- Depth/type of control   – What is important to the business *now*
- Asking for help   – and using it, ask rather than tell
- Levels of detail   – Too high in the organisation
- Reward mechanisms   – Promotion, pay
- Representation   – Unions, staff committees
- Organisation   – Size, multiplicity, is it geared to today's needs?
- 'Crutches'   – Functional groups
- Imposed demarcations   – Union or company inspired

The testing is simple: are the checklist items necessary and should they be the same as when they were established? As examples, meetings were often made routine in a time before computerised data was provided. Are they still necessary or has the new technology overtaken their need? Asking 'Why are we meeting?' or 'What is the aim of the meeting?' is an effective way of establishing real need. Daily production meetings might have been necessary when the leader needed continuous up-to-the-minute information because of his style; however, if the new style is to support trust and delegation perhaps this daily check is seen as counterproductive by those you are trying to influence. 'He says he wants to delegate but he still only trusts us for 24 hours'.

Similarly, if the accounting or control systems still project an era when management made all the decisions, then retaining the system will retain this flavour. Perhaps sales are shown only in volume and value terms – again established when growth was continuous – whereas the name of the game now is market share and competitive drive. This will only be felt by people when the company measurements are seen to reflect this new drive; talking about it without measuring it will rapidly build cynicism.

Are reward mechanisms out of date? Are they based on time-serving principles? Is risk and innovation rewarded? If they are not, if the reward for risk is not higher than the penalty for failure then the culture change of encouraging innovation will never get off the ground.

In so many companies, management speak of the need for innovation and cannot understand why it never takes off. The answer lies invariably in the perceived reward system: the element of risk-taking is not seen to be rewarded, yet the penalty for failure is often seen and heard. In this type of environment, a heads-down mentality will flourish and promotion will be seen based on failure avoidance rather than positive achievement. The corporate man excelling in company politics develops, as is often seen in large companies or the civil service.

Employee representation is often unchanged from the times when union structure was more dominant and necessary, exemplified by union consultative committees or works councils. With new communication drives this type of forum may be obsolete in terms of information flow; indeed, as we have seen earlier, all *new* information should pass down the line and not via such bodies so as not to undermine supervision. So what is their purpose? Perhaps they should be curtailed back to their prime purpose which might only be wage negotiation. If the meetings are held more regularly than the real need dictates, significant time will still be spent in the activity – time that is better spent at work for management and men alike.

The organisation itself may be fixed, perhaps based on a size and scope of business completely different from today. In large companies the 1960s saw a profusion of functional departments: Employee Relations, Personnel, Public Relations, Treasurers, Accounting, Office Services, Purchasing, etc. With the new concentration on business segment management, many of these may be superfluous yet they remain in being and often in size as they were. A key sign of change for an organisation is to see how its structure has altered; indeed, it is probably worthwhile to make a change in this area to make a public point – the status quo is being challenged. Accountability for actions can easily be dispersed in a large functional organisation as so many groups have to endorse or support a decision that the real accountability is lost. The functions provide a 'crutch' in some areas. Industrial relations problems should be solved in the line organisation, yet they can be passed on to employee relations and in the process accountability for the problems quickly becomes dispersed. The questioning in many companies is long overdue.

Finally, with this critical questioning the issue of demarcation must be raised. There are two demarcations in a company: one usually protected by trade unions as they historically were charged with this role; the second generated by the organisation itself. Inter-trade demarcation is usually highly visible and managements quickly recognise it; organisational demarcation is often less visible and much of management does not wish to see it. By drawing an organisation chart and placing people in boxes, the first big step in demarcation has been taken. The box – the department or function – begins to override and can take precedence over the company as a whole. Audit, accounting and public relations groups often appear in this category.

As an example, audit's function can become so strong as to limit the business itself, the achievement of good audit results becoming more important than achieving business results. Of course, business must be properly conducted with the right accounting, management and ethical standards. However, audits can often suggest areas where improvement is required without relation to the business itself. This is counterproductive and can act to reduce personal responsibilities in a business that needs an increase in this area if it is to succeed. Classical symptoms of such problems are a preponderance of systems, multi-reviews of ideas or actions and a fixed response attitude to problems – for example, an employee is found to be stealing, the system changes so as to prevent that incident happening again and the whole organisation is burdened with some new review or paperwork requirement. In a more balanced environment, the individual will still be punished but it will not be assumed necessary to change an entire system on the assumption that everyone else will similarly transgress. Taking the entire company down to the lowest denominator will have a significant impact on the perceived level of trust in a company. Do you start with the premise that your company, your people, *yourself* are honest and trustworthy or not? The transparency is total!

So the challenge is from leader to employees and vice versa. Both directions of challenge have impact, but we have seen how the leader's own style, together with company systems, set the environment within a company. In the challenge process, these two areas bear the initial pressure of change and open demonstration in these areas will allow people to gauge the seriousness and intent of the activity before joining in wholeheartedly themselves. The challenge, whilst initiated by the leader in terms of defining the purpose of the organisation and its goals, rapidly becomes one directed at him and his management as employees themselves check to make sure the interest, purpose and commitment is genuine before committing themselves.

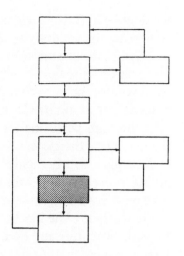

13

CHANGE

If we recap for a moment, the purpose of the change process is to:

- Align people behind the company's mission.
- Thereby reproviding a purpose to work.
- Thereby allowing each to give of his best.
- *Thereby releasing the hidden potential available in everyone to achieve peak performance for individuals and for the company.*

As we have seen this can only be achieved by creating the whole environment to support this activity and this is the initial challenge for management. Response will come from individuals after an incubation period, but the process depends for its success on it being a willing, not forced process. You cannot force people to give of all their talents and skills, they have to want to do so.

In striving for the release of this huge potential it is worth remembering the size of the jewel that is being sought. The difference in productivity, in achieving a state where everyone contributes to the best of their ability, can be very large. Leyland increased productivity in terms of cars per employee by 400 per cent, and Jaguar have even surpassed this percentage increase. Yes, new investment has helped but without attitude change whereby employees contribute to the process, the gain would not have been so high. British Steel have moved from the bottom of the international productivity league to be amongst the most productive in Europe and one plant in Wales is now close to world leadership in productivity. As we have already seen, the Washington tyre plant of Sumitomo is now an example of high productivity from its previously laggard position. So the list grows, and what is remarkable is that productivity gains can be measured in percentages of hundreds, not fives or tens. It now becomes clear why the high-performance companies can so easily out-perform the average – their cost advantage can be enormous.

This gain will be achieved directly as a result of individuals giving more to their work, and indirectly in supervisors and managers spending less time (up to 80 per cent!) in checking the work of others. The key to the process is creating space for people to contribute fully and then to move to an era where *people work to their own standards of performance*. In reality people in each organisation already work to their own standards. Companies try to impose standards but these are always superficial only. For example, a time clock makes people spend a fixed time at work but does nothing to force them to use that time effectively. A fixed-speed production line forces people to carry out a given task in a fixed time but does nothing for the quality of how the work is carried out. People are naturally inventive, and if their attitude to work is one of being forced they will not willingly give of their best, and indeed will be inventive enough to ensure they are not seen to underperform.

The change will come by accepting people already work to their own standards but by providing a purpose in work *to raise their personal standards*. The aim is to repeat the Japanese response to quality problems: fewer inspectors, more responsibility given to and felt by the line workers and relying on their standards rather than imposing inspection standards. Prevent the problem, do not work on catching errors – this move to self standards of work is very effective. It's worth examining the *quality issue* in more detail as this typifies the fundamental shift in thinking and practice that change can bring.

Quality – *The Special Issue*

In recent years much effort has been put into the improvement of quality as competitive standards in this area have increased. The Japanese have for ten years lead the world in quality, and we can learn from a comparison of their approach to that of our own industry.

Many Japanese companies operate with two clear strategies, both linked: minimum inventory levels and minimum product quality inspection. Their belief and practice is to give the producers – the line workers – accountability and responsibility for quality standards. Their efforts are concentrated on ensuring that the line worker understands the need and importance of quality and, as we have already seen, that he feels purpose in his task so that he works to high standards imposed by himself rather than the company. He feels his work is an important contribution to the company and therefore effectively becomes his own quality tester. He concentrates on 'making it right first time' rather than the system finding his errors through quality inspection by someone else.

This technique dovetails with minimum inventory holding. With the confidence in making it right first time less stock need be held as the time lag between an order and the certainty of producing on-grade products is minimised. Clearly, besides the customer's increased confidence in their quality Japanese companies gain by minimising the costs of holding inventory and those of an army of product inspectors.

Contrast British industry's strategy: with little effort applied to setting the right working environment, in communicating with the workforce, in explaining the need for quality, or making the line workers feel accountable for their own work, we have had to rely on that army of inspectors to try to catch the quality deficiencies arising from slipshod work. So we have put little effort into the production process and have had to put in excessive monitoring resources. The inventory-holding is naturally much higher as you cannot be sure of making it right first time. Costs are higher as a result and a significant competitive edge is lost.

Let's see how these differences appear side by side:

	Japanese	*British*
• The work environment	Right	Wrong
• The importance of work	Right	Wrong

	Japanese	British
• Self-responsibility	High	Low
• Make it right first time	Yes	No
• Production inspection	Low	High
• Recycled product	Low	High
• Offgrade product	Low	High
• Inventory level	Low	High
and		
• Product cost	Lower	Higher
• Customer satisfaction	Higher	Lower
and		
• Sales potential	Higher	Lower

As customers we have all responded to the Japanese initiative. From a reputation for making low-quality copy-cat products in the 1950s and 1960s which were scorned, we now confidently buy their products for their high quality. From video equipment to motorcars, they have reversed their image and their fortunes.

Contrast this awareness and change with the previously discussed example of Jaguar: a car purchased for its quality, but its image in the 1970s and early 1980s became one of consistently low quality and sales declined steeply. (In America in the early 1980s it was said if you wanted a Jaguar, buy two: one for the road and one for the spares.) Little wonder sales rapidly fell with this image. However, it took the danger of a virtually bankrupt company to alert the management and for them to convince the workforce of the need for quality. Now the company is again selling on quality and achieving success. It is a pity parts of our electronics industry did not learn the same lesson before their demise. Perhaps the difference in strategies helps explain why parts of our automobile industry today continue to struggle to hold their markets whilst Nissan are investing to increase their market in the UK.

But this is not the end of the quality saga. The most recent changes have increased the intensity of the quality battle yet again.

Many companies are now demanding consistency in their raw

materials *not* based on quality control but on process control. This requires the raw material producer to demonstrate his understanding of his own manufacturing process and specifically its impact on his product quality. Having determined the process variables which affect quality, he then has to have a control of the process and these variables of sufficient accuracy to ensure the product is totally consistent. Very often the 'tightness' of these variables is set so that product consistency becomes very good and effectively the specification of the product becomes much narrower in range. By definition, through control of the *process*, the *product* quality is assured automatically. With process control it is less necessary to test the product and the purchaser is often willing to forgo all testing thereby saving costs.

This radical change in approach would be beyond many of our companies, though it already is part and parcel of doing business with many US and Far Eastern companies. Indeed, although process control, in terms of demonstration and guarantee to a customer, may be a recent development, high-performance companies have sought quality guarantees for years. Marks and Spencer have always purchased to the highest of standards and reserved the right (and use it often) to 'audit' a producer's factory at any time to check that his process was up to the same high standards demanded of the product. They have as a result established a position in the food market by selling on quality and finding the customer responds readily to buy on consistency.

Michelin, whose tyres have always been leaders in durability and quality, have demanded intense quality control in their raw materials all the way back to the 1950s. However, they achieved this by having tighter specifications than the rest of their industry and by reinforcing quality at every opportunity. For example, if they experienced a quality problem themselves and traced it to a particular raw material, which perhaps was purchased from ten companies, then the lowest-quality supplier of these ten lost their business; if the problem continued, the next lowest and so on. This created effective indirect pressure for suppliers always to keep their own quality high and avoid being bottom of the quality league. Of course, by these methods Michelin were buying consistently high-quality materials, and other tyre producers were receiving the less consistent material – a double-edged advantage.

So the rules are changing quickly and quality is becoming an ever more important element in the markets of the world. How much of an advantage will be gained by those high-performance companies who already have committed workforces and managements will be obvious. Those without will have to change to compete in this environment, but it requires a complete change of approach from inspection to guarantee quality to process control and making it right first time and next time and next time. . . . The wheel has turned right back to the historic craftsman producing his goods to his own standards without any quality inspection by a third party – the responsibility was all his. Indeed, this last theme is being utilised today with 'ownership' demonstrated by a product having the name of the line worker or his shift shown on each lot number. Individual or group ownership of quality – it has a remarkable impact on a purchaser.

Yet the story is far from complete, and even more improvements to quality will occur in the future. But they will all be in the direction of personal ownership of the issue, reinforcing the need to create an environment and an organisation where the individual's contribution and responsibility are paramount.

Returning to the main theme of this chapter – Change – besides the environmental improvements suggested, *new reward mechanisms* will have to be found to help this process. Linking pay to company performance, group performance or individual contribution will become necessary as part of the change process. Our best competitors already do this and only our rigidity has prevented it occurring yet in the UK. It will have to happen. Strangely, many companies accept this need at executive levels where it is presumed people can *choose* to give of their best and therefore need encouragement in reward; no wonder there is a great divide in attitudes below these levels where it is not seen to be necessary. Tomorrow's world will recognise that the motivations below executive level are the same as those at that level; there is no divide in attitude, we are all common in this process, only history and treatment has caused the divide.

The change to working to your own standards, of *self-responsibility*, is the key to the process. Unfortunately most companies deny self-responsibility rather than reinforce it, and here are a few ways this occurs:

- Appraisal process   – Vague, are you valued?
- Lack of praise   – Embarrassing
- Lack of communication – Is your job meaningful?
- Lack of purpose   – Is the future worthwhile?
- Organised in big units   – Low identity, impersonal
- Tight job definitions   – Demarcation's breeding ground
- Inconsistency   – Lack of trust
- Tight control   – Avoids failure, limits success
- Tight departments   – Staff demarcation

Let's look at this list in more detail. Appraisal and performance feedback are the most important. If we are to move to a self-responsible system it is essential that management techniques improve to achieve this. Objective or goal setting has to be precise, more time will have to be spent in agreeing the aim of a piece of work, and equally more time must be spent in the feedback of results.

It is no coincidence that, as we have seen, apparently unmotivated people in work often have very active external lives. This is not only because they have a purpose to such activity, it is often because they understand what they are trying to achieve and can clearly see the results of their efforts. Conversely in work, it is often never explained what the goal is nor whether eventually it has been achieved. So to achieve results inside work on par with outside, the simple trick is to repeat the external conditions within work. Already we have talked of purpose and its provisions in work and now we see the importance of setting goals and continually providing feedback on performance.

Imagine playing football with no goal posts and then never announcing or knowing the score at the end of a game. The sport would die overnight. Yet this is exactly what is often done in work. People are unaware of their own goals or their team's goals and never get told whether they have succeeded or failed. In some companies an annual appraisal pretends to be the mechanism of feedback; however, this is generally too vague and imprecise. The analogy is of a team never knowing their individual match results but just knowing at the end of the season that they finished tenth in the league! Feedback needs to be continual in work as on the football field.

So the new management or supervisory skills will be setting and agreeing clear goals, facilitating and conselling to help their achievement if necessary, and feeding back results. It will not take more time than today's pseudo-review system, but will be continuous and effective. The process will be clear and precise, not vague and embarrassing, and it will have significant impact on performance. Every job is describable in terms of goals – if any is not then it is only because the man and his supervisor have not spent sufficient time thinking about the job. Just like a football game, without a goal there is no purpose in work.

In the process of giving feedback, a manager's job is to give praise. This does not have to mean money; we are talking of the little signs that say 'well done' and show the manager cares and values the contribution. As a nation we are embarrassed by feelings, but are we really? At home and in life outside work it is usual, it is only in work that we become stiff and afraid of people. A good start is to commit to saying 'thank you' at least once a day. Seek out the opportunities and try to find the people whose work is more routine; if you go looking, you will find the opportunities. Thank the secretary, the tea lady, the canteen assistant, the window cleaner; just watch service improve as you do.

If you are able to, use touch as an additional signal – like thank you, it shows that you care, and if you care so will others. When working overseas I used to wonder why other nations, the French and Belgians particularly, shook hands daily. Now I realise, like the West Indian greeting of 'I see you', it is a daily expression of recognition, individual to individual, and has great importance. The hands-in-pockets, no-thanks British style projects coolness, aloofness and, perhaps most damning, care-less. Start working at your personal style of involvement and care.

As the thrust to self-responsibility is fostered, communications and purpose in work have to be provided to ensure the individual feels he, his work and the company are worthwhile and meaningful, so that the raising of his standards has value.

An organisational deterrent to effectiveness is work group size. The smaller the group, the more personal and the better the individual's identity. Even if work sections cannot be made smaller, task teams can be created to produce the gains from high-identity working.

Recently, with pay scales set by points systems dependent on work responsibility, complexity and size, there has been a trend to define jobs over-precisely. Every definition increases the risk of demarcation. Definitions limit what you can do, they are usually non-enabling. We are seeking an enabling environment where the limits of contribution are not set. In this context tight job definitions often precisely describe those limits of contribution. Better to set out the purpose, the goals and leave the individual to achieve without encumbrance.

On the shop floor, demarcation is generally very visible – a tradesman can not cross another's skill area. Many training and apprentice schemes teach a limited amount of allied skills yet in the workplace little of these are usable. However, with a purpose provided and an environment created to allow and support working across boundaries, the productivity gain is very large, given that much working of multi-skill groups (with demarcation) creates wastage through overmanning or waiting time. The analogy, however, in staff jobs should not be overlooked. Similar limits on work, often implied by the company's organisation structure, are just as effective at reducing productivity.

Finally a review of *control* is recommended to help establish the environment to support the change to peak performance. Control is often apparent at too high a level – too far displaced from the work it is controlling. This is a symptom of under-delegation where trust levels are low and motivation and job fulfilment similarly depressed. Detail follows control and it will be found that senior management has a level of detail out of proportion to their level. Decisions are referred ever upwards, far beyond the level where full information and judgement are available. Another symptom of such organisations is that the phrase 'I don't know' is never heard; it is assumed that competence is reflected in total knowledge of all minutiae and the culture set from the top pulls details up the organi-sation like a vacuum. Action is stifled, many more decisions than necessary are referred to higher management, and delegation, trust and job satisfaction are low. A reversal of this process is necessary to give people space to contribute and perform to their maximum. Clearly this change can best be effected by change of style at the top, or it may even require change of the person at the top.

To be effective change, like challenge, must be a two-way process. Demonstrated change at the top is necessary before people can respond themselves. Therefore, many of the features discussed in this chapter require change to effect attitude change in those lower in the company. The signal of change has to be observed first and in this process the leader will be signalling how much space is to be created. Again, therefore, the process is driven and led by those at the top of an organisation with the ability to show behaviour shifts by example and who have the power to change company systems to create the supportive environment for the process.

We have talked of leadership style and the comparison of leader and manager; let us now see how organisations can vary, from the heavily controlled at one extreme to the fully contributive at the other:

	Controlled company	*Fully contributive company*
Atmosphere	• Impersonal.	• Caring.
	• Task-oriented.	• People-oriented.
	• Formal.	• Informal.
	• Management by appointment.	• Visible management presence everywhere.
Communication	• One way – downward.	• Open two-way flow.
	• Little feedback upwards, discounted if it exists at all.	• Action is seen from feedback.
	• Feelings not mentioned.	• Feelings expressed.
	• Hard facts/data.	• Data used with feelings.
	• Notice boards are communication.	• Notices confirm information.
Structure	• Rigid.	• Flexible – lots of task forces.
	• Committees everywhere.	• Less permanent structure.
	• Rule by law and rules.	• Fewer rules, more trust.
	• Hierarchical.	• Multi-level task working.
	• Tight job definitions.	• Roles defined not jobs.

	Controlled company	*Fully contributive company*
Management	• Respect through position expected.	• Respect through *style* and achievement.
	• Little informal walking about.	• Lots of informal contact.
	• Control people by hierarchy.	• Develop people.
	• Low tolerance for the ambiguous.	• High tolerance for ambiguity.
	• High energy at top, less at bottom.	• More even involvement throughout.
	• Mechanistic decision making.	• Decisions made on problem basis.
	• Decisions rarely reversed.	• Decisions tested frequently.
	• Low risk-taking.	• Experiments encouraged.
	• Errors are to be eliminated.	• High learning from errors.
	• Rigid departments; little interflow.	• Flexibility based on problem-solving.

As can be seen, as trust and delegation flow down an organisation, the organisation becomes more people-dependent and more flexible to the business needs. Rigidity of thinking and structure decline and time is released at a rapid rate so that people work more effectively in their *own* work areas rather than spending time in the cross-checking of other people's work or decisions. People's strengths are better utilised and with a less rigid structure flexing occurs to change as the business requires change.

A feature of rigid organisations is having the same structure as perhaps twenty years ago – management is less able to see the need for differing priorities and is unable to cope with the hierarchical problems involved in changing department sizes or scope. Indeed, much energy in these organisations is wasted in protecting the status quo. Resistance to change is often highest at the highest levels – by definition existing top management has succeeded with today's rules and environment and they, there-fore, have the most to protect by maintaining the status quo. No better example is presented to us than by Government and the Civil Service!

An interesting check question is to assume the management decides on a new action plan: do those people to be involved in the work ask *when* (is it required), *how* (is it to be done) or *why* (is it needed)? All 'when' responses spell extreme danger, 'how' and 'when' indicate a danger but some 'why's' signify a free atmo-sphere in which people can ask and, if answered, will work more effectively when the need is understood. Many management deci-sions never try to explain why – they often explain when and even how!

I briefly referred to an example of this in Chapter 1, that of Jan Carlsson, when he was new in SAS. He asked one of his managers how much it would cost to get SAS from the bottom to the top of the punctuality league in Europe. His manager came back and told Carlsson that, in his own area of responsibility, it would cost eight million kronor and he then started to explain what the money was needed for, to justify the expense. Carlsson stopped him and said he had the money – but he did not want the detail of how it would be spent. For eight million it was justified.

The manager was taken aback as he had been used to a detailed review, not only of why, but how, when and what! The job was carried out, SAS went to the top of the league and only a fraction of the money was eventually spent!

Under the old style all eight million or even more would have been spent because the 'how' would have taken on an impor-tance, an accountability of its own. But this new style gave space as the work had a spending limit but no other detailed accountabi-lity. The result was that the people involved found innovative ways of working and of saving money, ways that would have been stifled under the previous environment.

So we have seen how the company structure and environment have themselves to change to signal the company's readiness to accept new methods of working. By looking at the way that the company operates in terms of how people are guided you can get a useful insight into the atmosphere in the company.

Imagine the company as a spring; if it is held tight by feudal management and many unbreakable laws, for example, the energy remains in the coil. But if you have clear vision and values and people align to these, you can dispense with many fixed rules, safe in the knowledge that efforts will be applied in the right direction and enormous energy is released into useful work:

HIGH: RISK, INVOLVEMENT
      INNOVATION, FLEXIBILITY

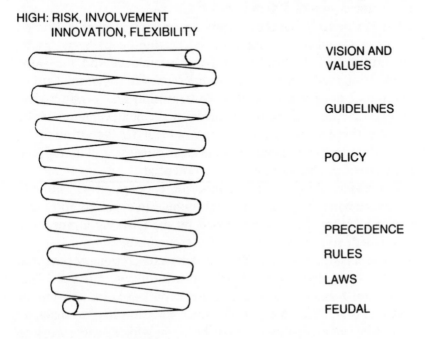

VISION AND
VALUES

GUIDELINES

POLICY

PRECEDENCE

RULES

LAWS

FEUDAL

LOW: RISK, INVOLVEMENT,
     INNOVATION, FLEXIBILITY

Each one of us has ability and potential which is only partially used at work. The unused part may be called the discretionary potential. This very simply is defined as the difference between 'what I do' and 'what I could do'. This cannot be forced from people, they *decide* whether to give that extra potential themselves.

Remember the Falklands conflict example, illustrated in Chapter 1. The country found a united purpose for a time and people up and down the country gave of their full potential, instead of the normal partial potential, with incredible results, similar to the example of the work on the QE-2. In understanding why this could happen it is important to understand the temporary environment created. The purpose was clear, the normal working rules of demarcation and control were removed, and people fully contributed to the prime purpose, putting the work above their own self interest. The result, a productivity and effectiveness gain of 500 per cent.

The key point is that the atmosphere or environment facilitated the process, and the spring uncoiled, letting people's energy be fully utilised. That brief period was soon over and the same organisations and same people slumped back to the normal atmosphere and normal low level of contribution and productivity. Strange that we took so much pride in the achievements of the period without asking why we could not achieve it continuously. The difference? In normal work no clear purpose and no tapping or release of people's discretionary potential.

So a review of how your organisation is operated will quickly determine whether your coil is tightly held in check by rules and laws or whether the coil is released by the enabling atmosphere established, so that people can fully contribute.

The aim is to release people's hidden or discretionary potential and to have it freely given to work towards the common good – set out in the form of the organisation's purpose, its mission or vision. To achieve this people must be allowed the space to contribute, an environment must be set in which people work to their own standards rather than applied standards, in the certainty that these personal standards will be higher and more productive if people are aligned behind the company's purpose.

The creation of space is management's responsibility – it can not be expected to spring up from below. In general, companies have proliferated rules and regulations to try to *force* work and standards in the absence of freely given full commitment. Rules *limit* people as they generally tell people what they *can't* do. However, a purpose *empowers* people by telling people what they *can* do. Easy to say, but management must start the process by giving away themselves – this creates space and begins the process of delegation, of self-responsibility, of working to own standards.

So define the purpose, own it by commitment, and then create space by moving to a self-responsible environment. Having done this, time will be created, time which can be used to check progress, listen to views, reinforce the purpose by walking about and getting closer to the employees. This donation of trust should extend to budgets, experimentation authority, and all aspects of work so that people feel the significance of the change.

Set out below is a checklist to review where in the process your own organisation might be today. The list is company-specific; however, these examples provide a thought-provoking checklist to see how much involvement is practised in your company. How much self-responsibility is being practised? Let's see the list.

Involvement Examples

1. Is absenteeism more than 2 per cent?
2. Do supervisors force work (as opposed to planning it)?
3. Do people have to clock on or off?
4. Is the safety programme seen as management's (as opposed to the employees')?
5. Do first line supervision have no budget control and authority?
6. Does management communicate via shop stewards (as opposed to the line)?
7. Is a central department responsible for industrial relations?
8. Is company or unit profitability not always given to the lowest levels in the company?
9. Are manpower targets not divulged to the lowest levels in the company?
10. Is your training effort less than 2 per cent?
11. Are jobs planned around men (as opposed to men around jobs)?
12. Are people in work groups of more than 20?
13. Are reviews for senior management checked by intermediate management first?
14. Are senior management rarely seen on the shop floor – informally, walking about?
15. Do senior management start work after shop floor people?

16. Is 'I don't know' never heard around the company?
17. Is typing usually checked by the originator?
18. At lower levels are letters, reports, etc., sent out under a supervisor's name?
19. Is there a bonus system for senior people only?
20. Is there a preceived 'us' and 'them' environment?

These 20 check points give a good clue to the environment in a company. More than 10 'yes' answers indicate a poorly involved environment where people are probably working to forced standards rather than their own. Full commitment to work will be low and the organisation will be a long way from high performance. The checklist gives a fruitful list of areas where change can be effected to change culture, and to begin the move to a fully committed work environment. Food for thought!

14

THE CHANCE OF SUCCESS AND HOW TO START

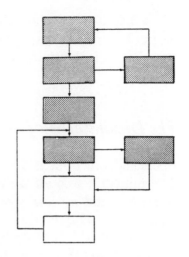

As we have seen throughout the preceding chapters, the key recurring features of an effective change programme are leadership, commitment, consistency and care. The process is transparent and those leading therefore, need to *believe* in what they are doing and *care* for their organisation and its people.

Much of the success will depend on the integrity, style and personal commitment of the leader(s). Indeed, the leadership's own purpose is probably the starting checkpoint as so many dramatic changes have been brought about by initiation from the top. Bottom-up change is possible but it is a very slow process and in most cases the process is ineffective as so much energy has to be dissipated in overcoming resistance from those in more powerful positions higher in the organisation.

Therefore, the likelihood of an effective change programme is firstly dependent on the leader – his personal commitment and purpose. If we now assume that the leader has the qualities and purpose to lead an effective process of change, what are the other features that will decide whether success will be achieved?

- The extent of dissatisfaction with 'today'.
- The clarity of the vision of tomorrow.
- The number of ways to negate resistance to change.
- The resources available.
- The clear idea of the first step.

These five features will largely determine whether a change in performance by releasing people's untapped potential is probable. Let us look briefly at them.

The Dissatisfaction Level with 'Today'

I personally feel this is the most important of the five. It largely determines the amount of energy available for the change process. If people, and especially senior management, are comfortable with the status quo, they will not only be highly energetic in protecting it, they will probably also put energy into preventing change. However, if people are highly dissatisfied the converse is true, they will have energy to overcome the status quo and effect change.

There has never been an effective leader of high performance with low energy. Change requires energy, although once occurring, change can develop its own energy. So the inertia has to be overcome and the critical energy needed to *initiate* change will depend, in the early days, on the applied energy. The greatest initiator of change is crisis – as we have already seen this is often the energy creator which enables people, organisations, even countries, suddenly to achieve peak performance. Crisis is perhaps the ultimate form of dissatisfaction with the status quo; a crisis implies the status quo cannot be maintained. Short of crisis then the dissatisfaction with the environment, the purpose (or lack of it), the performance, the progress or other key elements provide the energy to make change happen.

So the first requirement of an effective change environment is energy, which is often funded by dissatisfaction in what 'today' is.

The Vision of Tomorrow

The leader's purpose and commitment is of prime importance but equally the ability to translate that purpose – to lay out before people a clear vision of where the organisation is going – has significant impact on the probability of success. Many organisations have perfectly laudable directions but never achieve beyond the normal because they lack the ability to translate the purpose into a meaningful vision of where the organisation is aiming to go. It is the challenge and excitement created by setting down the vision which starts the pulling together process. The oft-quoted example of Kennedy's 'A man on the moon by the end of the decade' is a vision which is simple, challenging, explicitly clear, and became a rallying point for major achievement. Would the mission have been achieved without this elucidation of purpose? Perhaps yes, but surely at more cost and time without the enabling character of this rallying call.

Similarly, in crisis times great leaders emerge through their use of simple visions to bind people together, creating greater effort and inspiring them towards the goal. Churchill's ability to translate the need to the average person in clear yet inspired terms was one of his fundamental leadership skills. Similarly, through the passage of time great inspirational leaders have been just that – individuals with the skill and ability to inspire others through the clarity of their vision of what is required to be achieved and what that achievement is.

The Number of Ways of Negating Assistance

In the early stages of an effective change programme, as described previously, resistance will appear and the chance of success increases with the number of ways that resistance can be handled. Resistance is often not apparent in a high-performance environment because people are attuned to a common purpose. However, early in the process when resistance is met it has to be recognised, accommodated and negated by a number of means, none of which may involve the adversity of overcoming. For example, isolation of resistance is a useful technique. If a person feels particularly strongly against the change process it may be better to allow time for that resistance to reduce and put energy into limiting the spread rather than overcoming the individual resistance.

However, in assessing the probability of success, the ability to recognise and have alternatives for negating resistance is important. One of the key steps, of course, is to have 'management' recognise these alternatives to straight confrontation. In any win/ lose situation the loser may well harbour resentment that will work against his future involvement, which is exactly the opposite to the aims of the high-performance environment. Better not to get into the win/lose position. Yet how many public battles erupt which not only involve win/lose but have involved so much bitterness that the chance of a future of harmony is deferred for many years – and with it the chance of creating high performance. In these cases judgements may well have been made that the confrontation had to be precipitated as management and men had moved too far apart for alignment of purpose to occur. The bitter coal strike of 1984/1985 is probably the most public example that can be brought to mind.

The Resources Available

The second area of applied energy in the change process is that of resources: the more available, the higher the chance of success. This is, of course, one key reason why bottom-up change is less effective than top-down; the higher the power of the initiator to command resources, the higher the success potential. Resources in this sense can mean people, time, money or external help. Rapid change requires effort, as we have seen, in communicating, supporting, and throughout the entire process. The very act of commitment and leadership redistributes resources into what is seen to be important and this source of energy is a key to implementing change.

A Clear Idea of the First Step

Much of the change programme in organisations becomes self-perpetrating, but the initiation of the first step is all important. This is often a radical sign of a new intent and the bigger and more obvious the sign, the better. Again, thinking of effective programmes, many have started with a vision explanation, by a new leader, followed by a specific first step supporting this new direction. Although the complete change programme is often not plannable as it becomes dynamic by its own process, the first step needs to be thought through, as this is the critical checkpoint for the commitment of those involved.

As a simple example, high overtime environments are generally those with low productivity and high demarcation, as demarcation-inspired inefficiency leads to work not being completed in normal time. Management may set a vision of a demarcation-free work environment and, having recognised the problem, the first step might be to break the automatic link of uncompleted work and overtime. If people can achieve reward by working inefficiently through premium work rates on overtime, a ban on overtime might be a first step. The setting up and explanation of this needs planning and then the commitment to hold the position needs serious testing before announcement. What level of commitment is seen and felt if the new ban lasts just until the first major production effect?

The first step is critical: it is certainly the first and sometimes the last test of commitment!

So these five features can test the effectiveness of a programme and an organisation can be checked to see what the probability of success is likely to be. Try scoring from 0 to 5 against each feature below in your own organisation (0 is low, 5 is high):

- Dissatisfaction with status quo   0 – 5
- Clear vision of where the company is going   0 – 5
- Available ways to negate resistance   0 – 5
- Resources available to effect change   0 – 5
- Clear idea of first step(s)   0 – 5

If you score 15 or above the chances of creating effective change are high. However, of critical importance is your 'Dissatisfaction with status quo' score. If this is 4 or 5 then success is more likely. Remember energy to create change is the most significant factor in successful activities, and energy to drive the process to success usually comes from dissatisfaction or frustration with 'today's world'. A high dissatisfaction score, therefore, generally creates high energy and with it a high success probability.

Having briefly reviewed how likely success is, let us look at how to start a change process and summarise the early steps.

Establishing the Strategic Direction

The first step is to analyse your organisation, its strengths and weaknesses, and the industry and markets you operate within to establish the competitive patterns in order to be able to assess the opportunities and problems that result. The purpose of the exercise is to assess the company's position today and from this to establish where the company should be five or ten years in the future. It is important to carry out this work *as the first step* as it becomes the foundation of the future work both inside and outside the company. The future, by definition, is unknown but the company's *direction* has to be formulated within the realistic assessment of what its position is today and where its potential and desired position is tomorrow.

These positions can only be established by a realistic assessment of the company's strong and weak points, those of the competition it faces or could face, and a view on where the markets the company serves will move and change. This work may need external help, but senior management inside the company must derive the process, even if segments of information are provided from outside.

Describing the Company's Purpose and Values

From a knowledge and understanding of the right direction for the company, it is certain that the purpose of the company can be described. Remember, purpose (or mission) is not the objective in the business sense but rather a statement of what the company is in business to achieve – what is its primary purpose. Usually the leader and his close management are best placed to describe this purpose.

What is the significant binding reason for the company's very existence? From the examples given previously this is never a monetary objective nor often a numerical goal; it is usually a leading drive for the organisation – its reference is often 'being the best at' – when compared with its other competitors in the market. From the analysis of what prime aspects will cause a company to succeed in a particular industry and market this drive or need will become fairly obvious. It requires a fundamental asking of 'Why is the company in existence?'.

When described, the purpose has to be recycled to ensure it fits with the business direction required – little hope for either if they are not only comparable but a perfect fit. For example, there is no way a mission today for British Rail of 'providing the best possible service to travellers' can be compatible with an implied strategic direction of 'making a positive return'. The commercial strength of the direction will overwhelm the purpose – a conflict seen daily by most travellers. A cost-control style will reduce the frequency of railway carriage windowcleaning; a customer-orientated style will clean them more regularly!

Having defined the prime purpose, the principles and methods of *how* the purpose is to be achieved will set the values the organisation is to hold dear. The answer *to what and why* describes purpose, *to how* describes values. These will be predominantly people-oriented – how the employees will be consistently treated, how business will be conducted, how customers will be served. Again, when completed these will be recycled against the business direction; they also must fit. A useful tip in stating these values is to think of the company in ten years' time and to ask yourself or the senior management to describe how you or they would like or wish the company to be in terms of culture, employee treatment, environment, etc. The *values* these wishes represent then become obvious.

With a description of *direction*, *purpose* and *values*, the leadership will begin to gain commitment – acting consistently with these – by beginning the communication of them and by involving others in the understanding, interpretation and implementing of them. However, companies find the first steps most difficult – how to initiate the process, where to start?

Let's recap in more depth the techniques highlighted in Chapters 3 and 4: very effective ways of choosing the priority areas in which to start the involvement process to gain commitment. It starts with 'The continuum'.

Describing the Continuum

To achieve a purposeful and effective start, the continuum technique described on p. 32 will be found most useful. Pull a group of (initially) senior management together in a relaxed environment described in Chapter 3, and set out *what* the company needs to achieve, why it is important and how it is to be done. You will need to describe your analysis of the company, the competition and the market. From this you will describe where the company's strategic direction lies and the mission on which the company is setting out. All of this is required context and you should allow sufficient time for questions. Finally, you will describe what working environment you foresee to enable success to be achieved.

The latter part will require a description of the values to be used in the process. Set these down in a list of short phrases or single words: TRUST, TEAM WORK, RISK, AUTONOMY, etc., . . . whatever the key values are. Then set down their opposites, viz.

TRUST	DISTRUST
TEAM WORK	EACH FOR HIMSELF
RISK	SAFE
AUTONOMY	AUTOCRACY
etc.	*etc*

Have each member score where he feels the company is between these extremes today, scoring on a continuum of 0 to 100, where 0 represents (for example) Total Distrust, and 100 Perfect Trust. From the addition and averaging of these 'scores', one or two values will stand out as being farthest from the ideal today, i.e. with the lowest scores. These will provide effective areas to start change – hit the obvious first! But more importantly these are not the areas as perceived (just) by the leader; the group has identified them so they are 'ours' rather than 'his'. This ownership creates identity and commitment and as we will see later this can be utilised to provide energy to move the company along the continuum towards the environment of high performance. (By the way, this technique can be used in groups at any level in a company – a first line supervisor can use it, as well as the managing director, to start the process of involved change.)

Having scored the average of each of the values, now take the one or two values that are *least* present today (i.e. those with the lowest scores) and ask the group what events, styles, treatment, examples are present which show the poor value. Real examples will flow: take these and have the group work up an action plan of correction – actions defined by *who* will do them and by *when*. Commit to carry the action programme through and the process has started. Importantly, it will have started in the worst perceived areas, with the highest profile – and therefore with the most significant impact on others when corrections occur.

Task Forces

Involve others in these actions: set up task groups to implement some of the actions. Use people at different levels, from different functions, and ensure they feed back progress to senior management or the leader. Give publicity to these groups. Use people who will be effective. Unless it hurts to put a person in the group (in terms of the importance of his normal work), it is unlikely you are putting the right people into the task groups. By the use of these people you are showing the organisation very publicly how important this activity is – and make no mistake others will recognise this! In most organisations the setting up of task forces, whilst announced as an important activity, involves 'spare people' of less persuasive power and as employees measure the real importance by those involved they will perceive the issue to be less important. The trap is worth avoiding.

Another key aspect of task force working is to limit strictly the time to produce results, and when they are achieved disband the team. A time-scale no longer than two months maintains energy, momentum and visible importance. The act of disbandment then sharpens the activity, bringing real focus and speedy results. It also demonstrates that key people are not sucked into these activities 'permanently' to the detriment of their normal jobs.

As time goes by these powerful task force teams will be replaced and supplemented by *networks*. Networks are self-help groups giving their help, views and energy to common problems, freely across department boundaries. In the right environment many task groups will naturally flourish into networks. Again these activities mirror normal behaviour outside the work environment – for example, a sports club or church organisation will rely heavily on networking where the best of skills are applied to problems for a while and then new people with different skills progress the solutions. This is very much the way that the old village society flourished, and still does in rural areas of the country. Self-help based on the best available use of skills.

After task group working, management time for review and priority actions to follow up recommendations is mandatory. The fastest way to kill this evolutionary process is to have no visible action after the group's working. A clear demonstration of commitment by management must follow these activities. Utilise the fast task force and the fast follow-up and not only will you produce a high-energy, high-achieving environment, you will also never lack volunteers to undertake these activities. It may well be found that some voluntary element in the make-up of early task groups is very helpful. A volunteer by definition brings energy and interest and the act of accepting voluntary help again demonstrates an open and involved style of management.

Finally, in short-time task groups it will often be found that the recommendations are not fully tested. This is a powerful plus – as long as experimentation is then allowed. Involve others in the test; this will rapidly increase ownership, interest and commitment. It also positively shows that the environment of risk and innovation is being supported. So many companies plead for innovation from their employees yet never allow action without full analysis of any potential failure – hardly an example of innovation from the top. Innovation is never risk-free. So use the technique of experimenting too.

Whilst these initial steps are being taken, the other parts of the change programme can be commenced. Communication, consistency and all the other seven C's are all intertwined, but these initial steps give some ideas on how the process may be started. Let us just remind ourselves of the entire process:

1.   Set strategic directions.

2.   Describe purpose and values.

3.   Draw continuum of values (opposites).

4. Plot where you are today (profile).
5. Draw up priority list from 'worst' parts of profile.
6. Set task groups to work on priorities, then work solutions.
7. Feedback results, reset priorities.
8. Set new task groups to work on the next priorities.
9. Feedback results, reset priorities.
10. Recycle, repeat again.

This can be represented diagramatically:

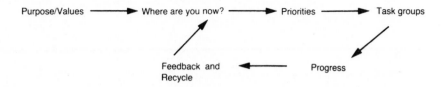

While this process is occurring, the leadership and management will be working all seven C's to increase ownership and commitment.

15

CONCLUSION

We have seen that to win it is necessary to have people caring. It means getting people to identify with the purpose of work and what they do so that they want to be committed. People without purpose have little constructive to give; their talents, abilities and energy remain untapped, and poor productivity, shoddy goals and unreliable service inevitably result. Effective leadership, by style and example, is required to create the environment for success.

As we have seen, the key to change lies in persuading people to give of their best. The difference between normal performance and the best performance is the discretionary potential available in everyone. It can't be forced from people, it can only be given willingly. However, if this willingness to put real commitment into work can be unlocked and released, then you can turn ordinary workers into extraordinary performers and the pathway to excellence and success is wide open.

We have seen examples of companies tapping into this discretionary potential with increasing success and remarkable results. To be competitive our industry cannot go on ignoring this resource.

But a moment of history may be relevant because we used to have that competitive edge, so why has it been lost? If we look back 80 or 100 years we see symptoms of high performance arising from commitment to work in three areas:

The Type of Work

People found a personal pride and identity in the end-product of their labours. A chair, a horseshoe, a thatched roof, a shoe – in most products, the craft skill was visible for all to see and admire. Indeed, today's customer seeks these goods from yesteryear at a premium. When the product was finished the craftsman stood back and admired it himself. Product quality was the craftsman's responsibility – no hordes of quality inspectors were necessary then. The standard of work was vested in the workman.

Apprenticeships were long and craft status well protected. The apprentice learnt his trade over time and that application was recognised by employers and employees alike. A few trades still retain the time and formality of long apprenticeships but generally they have been reduced in response to the needs of mass production. As the product began to lack individual skill and identity so man's pride in the product declined. So here is the first dilution of purpose which must be reversed: the loss of identity, pride and ownership in the finished product.

Size of Work Unit

The second loss from yesteryear is group identity. Companies were small and people worked in groups in which everyone knew each other. Often living in the same village or town, the group had enormous identity and purpose inside work and outside. As economies of scale grew, units became larger and larger, travel distances grew as car ownership increased so that people lived remote from work and, more importantly, from each other.

Work became depersonalised (could you name even the workers alongside you on a production line?) and the purpose of working with others grew smaller and smaller. Increasing size created a vacuum of identity, quickly filled as a vacuum naturally is – by people seeking outside identity to replace that lost in work. Clubs, pubs, churches, all thrived because people had to look outside to find what had been lost in the work place.

Ownership and Leadership

These small groups of yesteryear were led and often owned by individuals who lived in the same communities as the employees. The mill owner, although often allowing satanic work conditions, was known by all his employees and often seen outside work in the local church, fete or other gathering. He had identity. He walked the shop floor and knew most of his workers by name.

As units grew larger, multinationals grew up with ownership remote and even overseas, that identity with the leader disappeared. Worse, the management stopped walking the factory floor, knew few people by name and cared little that they didn't. That typical manager transmitted no feeling of care or concern: how could he? – remote from his people in a plush office, eating in a separate dining area and avoiding personal contact. The circle of depersonalisation was complete.

So another vacuum formed and was quickly filled. As the first natural identity with work disappeared, so people again switched identity to outside purposes – clubs, homes, churches all increased in activity. The UK is perhaps the top club nation in the world for the worst of reasons – we could not find a real purpose in work. Worse, inside work the vacuum was filled by other means. As management left the factory floor, trade unions thrived on the vacuum. In the worst of factories they replaced management entirely – unions set rules of work, of demarcation, the shop steward became the first-line supervisor or manager and union discipline often exceeded that of the company. In many factories the management almost needed permission to go on the shop floor, and as remoteness grew, knowledge of people declined and trust disappeared. Petty theft of materials or time grew – a sure sign that identity was lost. You don't cheat on your prime purpose but cheating your company became acceptable and open; indeed, it was even allowed for in productivity or product loss calculations. Sadly, it still is today.

So as the purpose in work, which we all naturally seek, declined so too did productivity, quality, commitment and care. This process happened to management and men alike. Mutual respect became mutual contempt in many organisations and the 'us' and 'them' culture grew.

Since the Second World War the process of decline has

accelerated. The process was gradual and largely unnoticed for a while as favoured access to the Empire and Commonwealth markets and worldwide product shortages meant our declining competitiveness had little impact. The renaissance of overseas competitors, particularly in war-damaged Europe and Japan, took time and during this time the mentality of government, management and unions was to return to the pre-war situation rather than foresee the new competitive drives and get ready to respond to them.

The oil crisis of the 1970s finally brought reality. Suddenly predictable and steady growth disappeared, over-capacity in production facilities world-wide became the new feature of most industries and competitive forces became dominant as producers chased markets where supply greatly exceeded demand. The UK's industries were ill equipped to join battle in this new game. Investment in new technology had been low: why bother in the 1950s and 1960s when demand could not be satisfied (remember waiting six months for a new car?) and, significantly, little progress had been made in achieving common purpose within companies. The productivity gains from an aligned workforce were not appreciated, seen or felt to be required – the country returned to the adversity structure of men and management with the annual struggles to divide wealth, personified by strikes and bitter public disputes.

The tearing apart and polarisation of companies in the UK was taking place whilst our competitors were quietly working on the pulling together and harmonisation of people at all levels. Armed with the productivity gains from these efforts, plus the strategic leadership which had renewed facilities and invested in new technology to achieve improved cost and service performances, the flood-gates opened and the domestic market was swamped. As an example, imported car sales grew from 5 to 60 per cent of the home market in 10 years.

Without the tools of new technology and equipment and a united workforce, British industry had to contract in the face of the new competitive forces and our manufacturing base shrunk alarmingly. But it was not only in cost performance that the decline occurred – service and quality attitudes also had sunk to an all-time low and customers began to exercise their choice in favour of the new suppliers. Buying a new domestic car in the

1970s entailed a major investment risk, the first service required the correction of a myriad of quality faults, whereas the German or Japanese car, produced at higher quality standards, needed little post-purchase correction.

Even 'quality' goods produced in the UK suffered because of uncommitted management and workers. Great cars, like Jaguar, lost markets due to quality erosion. Little wonder export markets disappeared. Indeed, to their eternal credit, the new management at Jaguar in the 1980s worked hard on quality and achieved a remarkable turnaround. Yet how sad, and what a condemnation, that throughout industry we had to feel the pain before change occurred. We can take pride in the examples of change, but only shame from the course of events that made the change so necessary.

As this book has tried to explain, to charter the turbulent waters of the future all a company's energies will be needed to fight and win the external battles. Time spent fighting within a company will be time not available for external issues. Strategic direction, based on accurate understanding of the company and its markets, will be necessary so that direction is correctly given, and then purpose and values will have to be communicated and accepted so that the entire company works to achieve the purpose *willingly* – thereby releasing people's talents and fully utilising their skills. The productivity gain from this alignment of purpose will be needed to compete effectively. There is no way technology or anything else can make up the difference if this alignment gain is not apparent.

We've seen that a way of achieving this new peak performance condition is by the simple system of the seven C's. The process can be summarised as:

1. FIND THE DIRECTION AND PURPOSE OF THE ORGANISATION

- Analyse the company, its strength and weaknesses.
- Analyse the industry, markets and competition.
- Define the external strategies.
- Define the internal core purpose (mission) and values.
- Check these for impact externally.

2. FOLLOW THE SEVEN C's

1. Core Purpose – the mission
2. Commitment
3. Communication
4. Consistency
5. Culture
6. Challenge
7. Change

These steps are all interactive and the entire programme will need close attention and visible leadership, but they can effectively cause radical change within companies and in their performance. The release of people's hidden potential to contribute to a common purpose is so powerful a mechanism that the individual and company performance improvement can be beyond belief.

The major challenge of such an activity is often seeing *the need for change*. The need arises from three sources:

1. *Competitors*

In many companies, battered by the new competitive pressures of the 1980s, the need is more visible now than ever before, but even so the depth of change required is not fully realised.

Some competitors already are achieving high performance – they are tapping that discretionary potential available but often unused in people. If you can tap into that untapped pool, the contribution change is enormous; if this is translated into productivity then a 100 per cent gain is quite achievable. In fact, as purpose and commitment return, the knock-on effects often exceed 100 per cent improvement – for example, quality improvements dramatically reduce the need for quality inspection, and the armies of quality inspectors grown up to try to contain the quality decline arising from attitude decline can again be dispensed with.

As competitors tap into this potential a very rapid and cost-effective change takes place. Instead of investing in improved facilities, companies often find they have discovered a non-capital way to achieve improvement. Again, as competitors achieve this, your company gets squeezed by their activities. Their production cost is less, their quality improves, their capital needs might decline – all forces bearing on you to change.

At the end of the day we all have to meet and then beat our competition. Government subsidies or trade barriers only delay the process; the end point is inevitable. With the efficiency improvements achievable by reproducing purpose in work for people – freeing their untapped potential – it is inevitable in time that all companies will have to try to tap into this source. The gains are so large that a company turning its back on the process will be totally uncompetitive and ineffective and will wither and die. So inevitably all will seek the improvements – if for no other reason than they are forced to do so by competitive pressures.

2. Tomorrow's Uncertainties

If competition will eventually force change, then so will tomorrow's uncertainties. In times gone by growth was predictable and sustained and even if an investment in new capacity were miscalculated, the growth in the market demand allowed the timing error to go unpunished and the capacity was quickly filled. Days of growth have been replaced by days of uncertainty. The external factors influencing business are now so various that demand curves are increasingly unpredictable to draw. War, social changes, inflation, government policies, currency fluctuations are ready examples of uncertainty. Companies can maintain a strategic direction but absolute levels of business are virtually unpredictable.

Yet how many organisations still have detailed long-term plans, showing volumes and prices to an awesome precision for 1990, 1995 or even 2000? They then compound the errors in these predictions by setting plans and strategies based on them. The only certainty is that they will be incorrect come the day.

In the face of uncertainty, organisations with inflexibility will fail. Response to the unknown requires total flexibility. Total flexibility because the range of error is enormous. The steel, airline, petrochemical, automobile and oil industries, for example, all overestimated demand by 100 per cent from 1975 to 1985. The reason: an unforeseen hike in the price of oil, which took it from $2 a barrel to $30+ a barrel in eight years. It was unforeseen and unpredictable – but the effect was traumatic.

With planning errors of 100 per cent, the oil industry itself built a capacity far beyond that needed to meet demand and consequently suffered as incremental sales were chased at any or even no profit level to try to fill expensive high capital production capacity. The days of 'dog eat dog' marketing. The same pattern and problems emerged in many other industries which all built massive capacity increases to meet demands that never materialised.

With this scale of uncertainty, three features are essential in organisations: *strategic direction*, a *slim organisation*, and *flexible people*. New planning methods will spend most effort on strategic directions and the need to define tomorrow, less cluttered by numerics, with perhaps just the next year numerically defined so that progress can be measured.

Leanness is essential as competitive pressures threaten the least fit first.

Flexibility comes from purpose, agreement and alignment of people behind company purpose. It is given by people, not forced by negotiation. Indeed, if you have to negotiate every change required in today's world, there would be insufficient time to do so as change is so rapid. Conventional piecemeal productivity deals are finished; they are obsolescent before their introduction. People's willingness to contribute and face different challenges free of artificial demarcation is mandatory today and will be more so in the next decade.

If you only negotiate change, by definition you are always chasing new needs. With flexibility through high performance, changes can be automatic. Fewer rules and more space for people to contribute – working to their own standards – is the key. Today people already work to their own standards – companies can impose very few – and by providing purpose those standards are raised in a way that applied rules can never achieve.

3. *People*

The last significant need for change is from people. We all need to feel cared for and valued in our work, at whatever level. Younger people today more readily question the assumed right of management to be right; they are in effect requesting purpose by asking 'why?'. The management-created vacuum will have to be filled – full value and fulfilment can not be achieved in an impersonal society. The care and concern in individuals, in groups and organisations will have to reappear.

If care is missing in management, then what right has management to criticise the same lack of care in their workforce? If a manager distorts his expenses for gain, then why shouldn't the factory floor worker take product or perform a 'foreigner' in work time. Both are stealing and exhibiting no purpose or care in the organisation. These common practices are changed by leadership and its style, not by ever-tightening audit and rules. Man has far more capacity to outwit rules than management has to write them. However, if purpose is reprovided, then cheating, whether at the top or bottom, becomes unacceptable by the society in work.

As society changes people will less readily accept the artificial rules of industrial society and strive for the same conditions they voluntarily seek outside work. Ownership, identity and commitment – transporting the conditions of home or club into work – would have a dramatic   impact on performance, moving the organisation towards high performance.

Companies are responding by recognising the importance of people. Less collective treatment, more personal space to consult; managers facilitating instead of giving orders; flexitime in work patterns; networks replacing top-down management – all features of the creative move to a new environment at work, leading to high performance.

So having seen some examples from history of why high identity was lost, and understanding why change is necessary and inevitable, let's finally remember that an organisation's own history can also affect the *rate* of change.

If the company is successful it is hard to see the need for improvement, particularly if little time is spent in looking at competitive or market forces. Perhaps the length of its history is relevant. A founder's views are often perpetrated well beyond the time when views should be related to new conditions. Historic responses can limit change: 'it worked in 1964, so it will work in 1994' is rarely said but often subconsciously followed.

Individuals also impact on the ability to change. Past experiences, conditioning and self-interest all have impact. Unfortunately the leaders of companies have often had to exhibit a 'cloned' mentality to succeed – to reach the top, behaviour in accordance with company 'norms' has had to be seen over a long period. The corollary of this is that when in the position of power, the leader or senior management can only think and act in the cloned manner, even though the new world requires action totally out of line with those past experiences upon which the cloning process was based. Individuals are similarly restricted by their historical understanding of company culture – assumptions on what is right, how to react, even whether to question. It is not unknown for the power appreciation to be so high as to limit thinking. Examples of 'the chairman thinks this' and 'woe betide anyone who argues or differs' are still quite usual in our companies. This can be reinforced by the data available in an organisation: is it directed at historic perspectives or primarily concerned with the future with different scenarios, competitors, environmental impact, etc.?

So we can see that to achieve change *all* aspects of an organisation will require examination. The need for change can be driven by crisis, or by intervention to achieve new business focus and direction as a pre-emptive step before decline occurs. The former is obviously often more rapid, but the latter is the real challenge of tomorrow's world. Surely, it cannot be necessary to deteriorate into crisis before the need for change is perceived?

Pre-emptive change is nearly always leader-inspired, and often follows a change of leader. New focus, direction and purpose are provided and the entire structure responds to these changes. The awareness of what the organisation itself 'says' to others, both inside and outside, is accurately perceived, understood and utilised. Business focus is reinforced by data requirement changes – what is measured, who is rewarded, what performance requirements are set out, which key people are appointed, what styles of leadership are to be reinforced. As we've seen, leadership style is a critical aspect of change and the effective leaders of tomorrow will:

- Be visionary.
- Act constantly to reflect their values.
- Act consistently.
- Be effective at leading change at all levels.
- Be committed.

Besides the structure of change – the seven C's – the key importance of leadership skill and style can not be overstated. The process of management for the 1990s will be so transparent that to be effective the leader must visibly believe in his direction, purpose and values. There is no half-way house, and indeed if the leadership is uncommitted or has motives that are short-term, it is probably better to maintain the status quo than attempt to implement radical change and performance improvement by these methods. Although such leaders may have short-term success – particularly in a crisis environment – the transparency will eventually produce a disillusioned and cynical response which may permanently harm the organisation. It will certainly make any successor's job many times more difficult in initiating any future change activity as he will first have to overcome a much larger barrier of caution and a much longer period of proof of change will be necessary before people (for a second time) respond to the new culture or style.

Many articles and books have been written on how to alter existing systems and attitudes within organisations. However, few have explained how to change attitudes and behaviour radically so that purpose is reprovided in work – a purpose to which everyone in the organisation can align and contribute willingly. This willing contribution enables the hidden discretionary potential within each person to be released and used for the good of the whole. As we have seen, release of this usually untapped potential provides a contribution so enormous that it can take employee and manager by surprise. It also is the key difference between the ordinary company and the peak performing company.

It not only enables companies to achieve excellence, it enables individuals to take pride in their own performance and contribution, thereby restoring dignity in work. It genuinely provides the uplift that occurs when people work 'to find the common good'.

This in turn needs a commitment and care for the organisation, its purpose and its individuals. Not transient, not artificial, but whole-hearted. This is the great challenge for management – for it is at the leadership level the change must be initiated. It has been British Industry's failing over the past half century, and we have paid the price for that failure. It is not too late to change but it requires effective leadership now. The challenge is: do you care enough – for your companies and your colleagues?

I believe signs are emerging – albeit in pockets dispersed through industry today – that we do care; we have to because without care we will inevitably decline to that perilous state in which we would be again under threat. But if we have to wait for disaster before changing, we risk all. Our epitaph may then become 'we did not care'. I hope, and believe, change will occur before this happens, and our industries will again seek the common good and rediscover that personal and collective pride and dignity in work which leads to high individual and company performance. The goal is clear, achievable and worthwhile: the question is, do you care enough to win?